MORE PRAISE FOR RECRUITING IN THE AGE OF GOOGLIZATION

"Recruiting in the Age of Googlization is a blockbuster story about what happens when the science of people, hiring, and emerging technology converge. If you are in any way responsible for hiring top talent, get this book today. It will save you a lot of time, money, and resources…and may even save your business. I can't recommend this book enough!"

Michael Spremulli, President of Chrysalis Corporation

"Recruiting in the Age of Googlization is Ira Wolfe's masterpiece – required reading for every CEO and leadership team. It's a prescient and practical book that will force you to question every response you make in our rapidly changing world. Whatever your job title or however small or large your company, this book will ignite the fire within you and your team to confront the challenges of this exponential change."

John Dame, Author, Executive Coach and Business Strategist

"Having read hundreds of books and interviewed an equal number of business experts on my Business Builders Show, I know REAL insight when I see it. The way we do business and especially the way HR operates MUST change. Recruiting in the Age of Googlization is one heck of a read!"

Marty Wolff, Executive Coach,
Business Consultant, Business Journalist

"Ira has exceeded all expectations in his latest book. His unraveling of the present and forecast of the future is scary accurate and yet practical for these turbulent times. The questions and solutions that Ira shares are essential for anyone expecting to lead effectively in this VUCA world. If you don't want to be left behind, I strongly recommend this book."

Kerry Goyette, President & Founder, Aperio

"Ira's ahead of the game again! The coming labor shortage: dealing with 5 generations in the workplace; and now the ridiculous pace of change. Whether you have one open position or hundreds and want your business to grow you better understand SHIFT & VUCA."

Scott Fiore, Vice President, TriStarr Staffing

"The *Future Shock* of our time. Wolfe not only spells out the un-paralleled pace of change today but also provides a guide on how to adapt and work it to your advantage."

Peter Dent, President, CDG Environmental and
Past Chairman, Da Vinci Science Center

"It is no secret that today's world is rapidly changing. Ira Wolfe makes this abundantly clear in his new book. He has produced a clarion call for paying attention to the exponential change that is occurring. Even better he provides guidance on how to deal with the change that all executives and human resources professionals should heed. As Wolfe says '...past success no longer entitles you to a future legacy.' My reaction to this book was to think 'Damn, Ira has written the book I wanted to write.' Everyone will be well served reading this book."

Mike Haberman, Consultant and Partner,
Omega HR Solutions, Inc.

"With *Recruiting in the Age of Googlization*, Ira has hit another home run. His knowledge of recruiting, hiring and managing todays workforce establishes him as the consummate expert in the field of human resources."

Steve Schulz, Publisher, Business2Business Magazines

"Ira Wolfe's *Recruiting in the Age of Googlization* offers business a powerful message: people analytics will determine the success or failure of employee selection and retention. He does a colorful job of introducing the reader to the disruptive power of exponential change then offers practical solutions that every organization can use."

Edward E. Gordon, Author of *Future Jobs*,
President of Imperial Consulting Corporation

"In this engrossing book, Ira delivers a penetrating analysis of exponential change and the challenges it presents to business, especially talent management. His examination of recruiting and analytics is an essential resource I will implement immediately and use going forward. *Recruiting in the Age of Googlization* is the blueprint for every executive who needs to recognize the tipping points of their industry and how 'disruptive technology' can be turned into an advantage."

Mark Walker, VP of Business Development,
Merchants Information Solutions

"We are faced with one of the most challenging recruiting markets in recent history (and I've been in the field for over 30 years.) Ira provides an excellent explanation of HOW we got here and WHY we are faced with such a challenge. We simply MUST change how WE go about recruiting if we hope to improve employee retention and organizational capabilities. Ira, as always, provides excellent support to demonstrate and show exactly why employers and HR are the ones that must change – not the candidate! Written with humor and in a style that anyone can understand, his latest book provides an excellent rationale for the change we must implement when seeking talent. Best of all, he suggests the right questions to ask to start the ball rolling to MAKE change happen!"

Karen A. Young, SPHR, SHRM-SCP, Author – *Stop Knocking on My Door: Drama Free HR to Help Grow Your Business*

"From the first time I met Ira, he has responded to new challenges with keen insight and innovative solutions. *Recruiting in the Age of Googlization* is no exception. It's an easy-to-read and practical blueprint for hiring managers and recruiters to compete for top talent in today's changing labor market."

Bill Schult, President, Maximum Potential Inc.

"This book is a boot camp for internalizing change! It is a bellowing call to recognize that the world's economy has two simple realities with a middle (consumers) that is indispensable. It is a sobering call to embrace the rapid activity, acknowledged or not, of infusing obsolescence and inadequacies in the pursuit of sales and profit. It is the dangerous dance between ignorance, indecision, and the lethal click that will determine the difference between thrivers and survivors. While the information in this book will not solve issues; it most certainly will create an urgency to recognize the continuous flood of emerging issues. This is a clear case for getting knowledge and above all, gaining understanding. Mental, physical, and emotional agility will be a constant dance. We must all dance like nobody is watching and work like everybody is waiting."

Ivory Dorsey, Professional Speaker, Facilitator, and Author

"Ira Wolfe is 100% on target with this book. We're investing more resources in extracting information from the "digital sea" than I could have ever imagined 5 years ago. But it's a necessity to stay competitive in finding top candidates and "being found" by them."

Kathy Cole, President, DK Cole Executive Search

"Ira's take on the future and the changes required to engage, hire, train and retain high quality performers is right on the money. I couldn't put this book down. This is a must-read with an abundance of takeaways management and HR can implement immediately. With *Recruiting in the Age of Googlization* Ira establishes himself as one of the authentic people management thought leaders of our time."

Terry Kile, Regional Director, Litmos

"Ira Wolfe has done it again. He accurately predicted the coming of the *Perfect Labor Storm* and in *Recruiting in the Age of Googlization* does a masterful expose of connecting exponential change with imminent employment and labor challenges. It is thought-provoking and a must read for senior managers and HR. It should be required reading for all managers, employees, and jobseekers too."

Martin Gilligan, Martin & Associates

RECRUITING IN THE AGE OF GOOGLIZATION

When the SHIFT Hits Your Plan

By Ira S. Wolfe
President, Poised for the Future Company
Founder, Success Performance Solutions

Published by Motivational Press, Inc.
1777 Aurora Road
Melbourne, Florida, 32935
www.MotivationalPress.com

Manufactured in the United States of America.

ISBN: 978-1-62865-464-6

Contents

FOREWORD

WHEN I MET IRA in 1996, I knew he was someone I needed to know. He wasn't just another expert in our industry but a visionary and thought leader for the future. I subscribed immediately to his newsletter and have read it religiously every week. It was just a short time later that I heard him present "The Perfect Labor Storm" and ever since, he has done nothing but confirm my initial opinion. Without his keen insights and friendship, I do not think I would have become as successful in my own business.

His latest work *Recruiting in the Age of Googlization* is an eye-opener. While reading it, I couldn't help but feel overwhelmed with concern for many of my clients. I do not believe they have any idea about how disruptive exponential change can be and how it is going to disrupt their businesses. One of my favorite quotes from the book is, "Exponential change doesn't play favorites. Each and every industry is in its path . . . The 21ˢᵗ century will be the equivalent to 20,000 years of progress at today's rate of progress." This unprecedented pace and scope of change requires executives of all organizations to shift and adapt their approach toward leadership, employee selection and retention.

No sooner did I think I finished writing this foreword when a headline caught my attention: *J. Crew's Mickey Drexler Confesses: I*

Underestimated How Tech Would Upend Retail. Drexler is a legend in the retail industry. He redefined Gap Inc. in the 1990s and turned J.Crew into a household name. But like so many other storied retail executives, Drexler finds himself and the organization he leads scrambling. "I've never seen the speed of change as it is today," he told the Wall Street Journal in May 2017.

Just a few weeks earlier, the prominent investor Warren Buffet announced he completely cashed out of Walmart stock. Why? The success of online shopping behemoth Amazon! In the same article, former Walmart CEO Mike Duke said that his biggest regret as CEO was not investing more in e-commerce to better compete with Amazon. Duke said, "I wish we had moved faster. We've proven ourselves to be successful in many areas, and I simply wonder why we didn't move more quickly."

Stories like these just keep coming. I worry how many more business leaders and government officials underestimate exponential change. The Age of VUCA (Volatility, Uncertainty, Complexity and Ambiguity) is here now...and Ira warned us years ago! Yet, many managers are still fixated on dealing with things like generational differences, especially how to manage the Millennials and Generation Z. In the Age of VUCA, generational gaps become just another "shiny object" diversion. The real issues confronting management and human resources are more complex than that and Ira does a brilliant job of addressing the problem and offering solutions in simple straight talk.

Today, how to prepare and deal with the massive disruptions coming from transformational change is an essential skill. According to Ira, "selection and development must be focused on identifying and building leaders with critical thinking skills, the ability to innovate, a passion for continual learning, resourcefulness, and adaptability." Companies, and especially Human Resources, must appropriate at least as much attention to the design, content, and marketing of talent acquisition as sales and marketing does to customer acquisition. Not utilizing all available appropriate tools including assessments for talent selection and retention and then analyzing the data is a mistake no company can afford to make.

The good news is that many organizations started using assessments and other metrics years ago to help them identify and grow future leaders. Unfortunately, few of them have started to use even basic tools to assist them in identifying what behaviors, motivators, and skills it takes to do the jobs, form teams, and fit in company cultures. It's time to SHIFT or die!

Recruiting in the Age of Googlization is Dr. Ira Wolfe's definitive work. As its simple truths begin to challenge your conventional thinking and upend industry and societal norms, you'll soon discover you're reading a business primer for anyone that wants to manage his career and run his business right. Today is not soon enough to start applying his insights, common sense, and wisdom.

Judy Suiter,
Competitive Edge, Inc., Founder & CEO

A Few Words From the Author

THIS IS MY FIFTH BOOK and it has been by far the most difficult to write. New emails, articles and videos highlighting innovative breakthroughs arrive in my inbox and on my smartphone screen with increasing frequency. As fast as I can put my thoughts and ideas on paper, something changes. It seems as if each time I refresh my screen, another disruptive breakthrough announcement appears. The world I thought I knew is constantly being shifted. The future seems to be paradoxically less certain and more ambiguous but filled with more promise and fascination.

Here is just one example in a typical day. As if the conversation about autonomous automobiles and trucks isn't enough to ignite disruption, an announcement about an "all-electric aircraft" turned up in my inbox.[1] The news about a "flying car" company, backed by Google-founder, Larry Page, arrived just minutes after I received my edited manuscript back from my publisher. Designed to operate over water and not require a pilot's license, the Kitty Hawk Flyer promises people will learn to fly "in minutes."[2] I just couldn't seem to get ahead of the news about change.

Then more alerts popped up on my screen. Advancements from CRISPR/Cas9's gene editing technology proclaimed real hope in the race to end cancer and cure debilitating diseases like Alzheimer's, Parkinson's, and diabetes. 3D printers produced a heart blood vessel for newborns, medications, and a car tire that never needs air or replacement. Someone even 3D printed a chocolate cake! And within the past week or so, I received a video about a new home being "3D printed from scratch" in just 24 hours. A straightforward analysis of all the news about change defies 20th century logic. That statement alone should be terrifying for most executives and business owners.

I started this most recent book writing venture as an update to my last book, *Geeks, Geezers, and Googlization*. Soon after I began rewriting it, I realized that I had failed to mention anything about the effects the tablet, specifically the iPad, was having on Millennials as well as older generations. How did I miss the product that almost single-handedly disrupted the personal computer industry and altered how millions of people connect to the Internet? It wasn't a mistake after all! The iPad wasn't introduced to the public for another year (2010). It was at that moment that I realized the biggest challenge that organizations and people face was the speed of "Googlization," not geeks vs. geezers.

Months of research, hours of interviews, and days of writing dozens of articles ticked away. The real story that needed to be told was no longer just about multiple generations working side-by-side or the acceleration of the pace of technology. The real story it turns out is about change. Not just ordinary change, but massive transformative change—the type of change that shifts everything we think we know to a different place. And it isn't just the scope of change we're talking about either. It's the rapid speed of change. It is accelerating so fast it has its own name—exponential change.

Exponential change means that the plans we had and proven strategies that used to work don't work anymore. You can throw more resources at it and you can throw more bodies at it, but whatever you do just stops working. The life cycle of products and services reaches obsolescence faster. Time-tested business models hit the wall. Exponential change isn't just a business problem either. The reliable pathways of education to employment are collapsing. The most popular in-demand jobs suddenly fall out of favor. Exponential change causes massive disruption that affects everyone's plans.

As you might imagine, reading, learning, and writing about change of this magnitude can take you down a rabbit hole with an endless maze of tunnels. The research for this book became my personal pursuit and passion for over two years. The book itself is also the culmination of years of entrepreneurship and a lifelong pursuit of understanding change. After a few unintentional detours, I found a place where the convergence of technology, jobs, and people meet. This place I fondly call, *SHIFT*. *When the SHIFT Hits Your Plan* became a white paper and eventually the subtitle of this book.

The journey in writing this book also inspired my TEDx talk—*Make Change Work for You*. Preparation for the talk and the ability to share my idea worldwide enabled me to meet hundreds of incredible people doing extraordinary things and changing lives. They have inspired within me optimism for humanity and an attitude of abundance I hope to pass on to you. I also hope this book inspires crucial conversations in our schools, at our workplaces, within communities, at the family dinner table, and on social media about the exponential change we're all experiencing. After all, exponential change has no boundaries. It affects everyone, regardless of age, gender, race, ethnicity, nationality, religion, or geo-location.

While the subject of exponential change could be a book in itself, that wasn't the only story I wanted to tell. The book is actually three themes in one. The first few chapters define exponential change and how it is impacting the ways we live, play, and work. I just can't emphasize enough how massive the scope of change is and the speed at which it is disrupting the status quo. Without this context, organizations and individuals may continue to plod along as if the future were coming, when it is really here today. It will be different tomorrow.

The middle chapters focus on a problem that has moved to the top of every CEO's list: how to attract and hire top talent. For the past decade, "recruiting Millennials" has been the overwhelming favorite theme for keynotes and workshops and a consistent challenge expressed by management. But the need to recruit "better" employees has matured from an inconvenience to a business strategy killer. Finding qualified workers isn't just a Millennial problem either. The convergence of exponential change and an ineffective recruitment process makes it impossible to attract talent from any generation – from the part-time student working his way through school to the mature and experienced executive.

The third theme is people analytics. Knowledge is power. Today, thanks to the convergence of big data, artificial intelligence, and machine learning, it's easier than ever to scientifically identify trends, spot behavior, and prescribe solutions. Using analytics is how a health care company can predict when patients with chronic diseases will need a particular drug on a particular day and save money for everyone. Big data is at the core of marketing, sales, operations, and logistics. It is becoming the life and soul of nearly every disruptor. Why not HR?

But data should not be treated like deity. Collecting and examining data is just a means to an end. Nevertheless, the results demand extreme respect. The analysis of data tells a story, one that is sorely missing in recruitment and talent management today. Hiring top talent shouldn't be a mystery. There's no reason to wait for months after the new hire's first day at work to figure out how well he/she will perform. Likewise, terminations—voluntary and involuntary – shouldn't be a surprise either. Employee training requires a huge investment of money, time, and resources. Its return on investment should hinge on people analytics, not hope and prayer. People analytics must be an integral process driving talent acquisition and management that reveals predictable and reliable outcomes. Organizations that learn how to harness the specific knowledge generated from the skillful application of people analytics will successfully navigate today's and tomorrow's environment of exponential change.

A few of you might be wondering why I didn't include separate chapters about retention and attrition, both huge problems for many organizations. It wasn't an oversight or a decision I made lightly. High turnover among staff and hourly wage employees is costing companies a bundle, and the involuntary departure of a key employee can be devastating.

Despite the need to alleviate the high cost and pandemic of employee turnover infecting many organizations, the solution won't come from more pizza parties and motivational speakers. The persistence of turnover isn't caused by a lack of knowledge but a lack of evidence and commitment to do what it takes to fix it.

I also didn't feel the need to provide information that most executives and managers already have. There are literally thousands of case studies, articles, and experts offering advice on ways to improve retention and reduce attrition. Besides, attempting to fix the problem without good people data and analysis typically amounts to using a Band-Aid to treat a cancer. Cloning a best practice works only when company cultures and a host of situational factors are nearly identical. Since that's a rarity, the copycat solution amounts to no more than a trial-and-error approach, and outcomes often fall short of expectations.

Alternatively, people analytics adds science to what has been traditionally a reactive and intuitive talent management approach. Whether it's increasing base pay, offering tuition reimbursement, or dangling motivational rewards, HR's modus operandi is mostly trial-and-error and requires a wait-and-see approach to outcomes. People analytics takes the guesswork out of the equation by identifying specific factors that contribute to turnover and attrition (and other business problems), thereby helping avoid mistakes before they happen and prescribing better solutions in advance.

The chapters on people analytics do, in fact, address turnover and attrition, just not in the typical way. Without good people analytics, the future of recruitment and retention will become an even more expensive and unpredictable proposition for companies.

I'd also be naive in suggesting that the chapter on analytics is anything more than an introduction. People management is a journey, not a destination. Predictive analytics, the heart-and-soul behind people analytics, is a tool and a process, not a quick fix. Nevertheless, analytics will help organizations zig when the world zags—and it will zag more frequently and unexpectedly! People analytics will become a company's best friend and asset; it's a burgeoning science with far-reaching implications for business. The analytics train however is leaving the station and it won't be making a round trip to pick you up later. All aboard.

INTRODUCTION

S HIFT OR DIE. It's that simple.

To make matters worse, humans suck at exponential change. We think when one thing happens it has only one effect. We assume we know all the dots and where they are. We don't. We assume connecting the dots will give us one answer. It doesn't. The reality is far more complicated. Each dot is a moving target. It interacts with other dots and how they combine keeps changing too. Each combination produces different effects that can impact what we do right now, fairly soon, in the near future, in the far future, and in the very distant future. Something that happens now can even impact the past by impacting our understanding of that past. This degree of complexity leads to a lot of mistakes that makes most of us uncomfortable.

But it's not just complexity that makes life more challenging and uncertain these days. Change doesn't just knock once and leave. Its persistent rat-tat-tat disrupts our lives; not just frequently, but continuously.

Like the old ticker tape and the modern day rolling LED banner, text messages alert us to breaking news stories. From sports scores to weather to traffic reports to terrorist attacks, updates pop up on our mobile devices and TV screens all day long. Many of the

messages get lost in the noise of our daily busyness. Others catch our eye and curiosity kicks in. We click to get more information. One day early this year (2017), my smartphone literally and figuratively lit up like a Christmas tree. Message after message kept popping up. Each one affirmed much of what I first forecast in 1999 – exponential change was shedding jobs and exacerbating an acute and persistent shortage of skilled labor. The events of that day embodied the convergence of exponential change, accelerating technology, and the digitization of jobs.

The first alert I received announced the impending doom of one-time retail powerhouse, Sears. Its stock had reached an all-time low as they announced plans to sell off their iconic brands, Kenmore and Diehard. Then just a few minutes later, former technology giant, IBM broadcast a headline that revealed its nineteenth consecutive quarter with declining revenue. Those announcements were followed with news about two more giant retail brands, Macy's and JC Penney, shuttering hundreds of stores and laying off thousands of employees. In the following days, The Limited, Payless, and Radio Shack released plans to lock their doors. As predictable as the sun rising each morning, the sun seems to set on another retailer that announces a series of store closings, layoffs, or bankruptcy.

Ironically the amazing announcement that Amazon would acquire the iconic Whole Foods came just a few weeks later. The magnitude of this business transaction is almost inconsequential compared to the size of its influence on things to come. At first glance it might seem Amazon is going into the grocery business. In reality what Amazon gets is massive data on more shopping habits. Could it soon acquire a 3D printing company to manufacture its

own products on demand and a drone company to deliver to your front door? Stay tuned.

Many people believe that the rise and fall of business in the retail sector is due to a failing economy. Certainly, the economy is not as robust as we'd like. Others blame the closures on fickle consumer trends that have simply run their course. Ordinarily, you might get away with either argument. But not this time.

The collapse of retail brick-and-mortar (and the jobs that go with it) is not a sign of a crumbling economy but a demonstration of how myopia blinds management to market disruptors and executive hubris suffocates innovation. It wasn't Uber's and Airbnb's business models that rocked the transport and hospitality industries but the iPhone and its apps that made them possible. That's the subtlety and nuance of exponential change. This wave of going-out-of-business is a clear and present failure to respond forcefully and quickly enough to a digital world. "Success sows the seeds of its own undoing, unless you keep rethinking how you succeed," is advice offered by Fast Company co-founder Bill Taylor.

Here's some evidence to back Taylor up. Since 2006, the value of Sears has dropped over 96%, JC Penney has lost 86%, Macy's 55%. Meanwhile, Amazon increased 1,934% and is on track to be the first trillion-dollar retailer. Its market value at the end of 2016 was greater than Walmart, Target, Best Buy, Nordstrom, Kohl's, JC Penney, Sears, and Macy's combined![3]

Online shopping offers the allure of a search that produces dozens of choices, one-click pay, and next-day or sometimes even same-day delivery. Brick-and-mortar retailers simply can't compete with traffic and parking delays, spotty inventory, mediocre customer service, and long checkout lines. The convenience and

experience of the online retail world has doomed brick-and-mortar retail. Automation didn't just doom one business or industry either but thousands of jobs too. According to a landmark study by Carl Frey and Michael Osborne, the retail salesperson's job has a 92% probability of being automated in the next decade.[4]

The SHIFT just hit the world of retail's best laid plans and best conceived strategies. It's as if management was comfortable pounding the keys on their manual typewriters when consumers were demanding texts and tweets. It was a shift that retail didn't see coming and wasn't prepared to span.

The demise of brick-and-mortar retail isn't just an isolated case study of the volatility in the retail industry. It's just one example of change that is impacting every industry. Exponential change doesn't play favorites. Each and every industry is in its path. It indiscriminately destroys battle-tested business models too. It carries massive implications for jobs, which is what this book is really about—how work gets done, people find jobs, and employers recruit workers in today's and tomorrow's environment of exponential change.

Let me go back to that day early this year when my phone was lighting up with news about SHIFT. The news wasn't all bad. Not all companies had opted to just lie down and wait for change to run over them. In its heyday circa 2000, the Goldman Sachs cash equities trading desk was packed with traders—600 of them to be exact. Fast forward 17 years, and they have discovered that four traders can be replaced with one computer engineer. Complex trading algorithms, some with machine-learning capabilities, have replaced nearly all of the equity traders at Goldman Sachs. This isn't a futurist's prediction; it's a present-day reality.

Today there are just two equity traders left, replacing 598 of their brethren with 200 computer engineers[5]…which is just a drop in the bucket compared to the 9,000 computer engineers on Goldman's staff. That's nearly one-third of all employees. Goldman already has set its sight on investment bankers. They have mapped the 146 specific steps taken by this group and plan to transfer these job responsibilities to automation. Goldman Sachs is not alone. The world's largest money manager, Blackrock, dumped traditional stock pickers for "quants" (quantitative analysts) who rely heavily on artificial intelligence and very sophisticated algorithms.[6]

The barrage of alerts just kept coming. The next text announced Bank of America's plans to launch people-less branches and a virtual assistant like Siri within the year. Their strategy includes, "literally automating every single thing."[7] FedEx followed with plans to launch an autonomous delivery fleet, thus demonstrating the convergence of autonomous vehicles, sensors, artificial intelligence, and robotics.[8] These same technologies can, and will, revolutionize the multi-trillion-dollar logistics market, affecting everything from the way people send and receive parcels to the global movement of large fleets of vehicles.

Executives and small business owners often tune out announcements like these because they get so focused on day-to-day business. The status quo acts like a powerful tranquilizer. They rely on competitors for news and industry associations to advise and protect them. That often leads to group think which throttles back the urgency to innovate.

Exponential change is so disruptive that even professional change agents can get caught flat-footed. The legendary American business magnate and investor, Warren Buffet admitted at the 2017 Berkshire Hathaway Annual Meeting that he "didn't anticipate how much Amazon would threaten the retail industry."[9] If Buffet missed it, how do any of us ordinary people have a chance? That's the danger of exponential change.

Daniel Burrus, founder and CEO of Burrus Research and one of the world's leading technology forecasters and innovation experts, believes: "People never think big enough."[10] That's certainly true when it comes to grasping the far-reaching effects of second- and third-level consequences. Disruptive technology doesn't just create ripples; it's a tsunami that generates tidal waves that reach far beyond what most people imagine or anticipate.

Consider the retailer that relies on daily commuters shopping on their way to and from work. What happens to them when more workers telecommute or self-driving vehicles change traffic patterns? With more electric cars, what happens when customers don't need to stop for gas, snacks, or coffee as often? What happens to government coffers when fewer gas sales and empty parking garages generate less tax revenue?

It's also more common – and maybe even more likely – to see disruption coming from outside an industry (outside-in) than from inside-out. More than a century ago, the "horseless carriage" – our beloved automobile – wasn't the innovation of the entrepreneurial CEO who happened to own a horse whip company. The transportation industry was disrupted by an outsider. At the time that type of outside-in revolutionary change was unusual. Today it seems to be the norm. "Big Blue" IBM used to be one of the largest and most innovative computer companies in the world. Today most young adults only know it as an information and analytics company – aka IBM Watson. The Kodak sign was everywhere. Today, young people ask "what's a Kodak?" Both companies were rocked from the outside-in.

Here's another recent outside-in disruption: For over half a century, Honeywell dominated the U.S. thermostat sales market. With nearly 39% of U.S. thermostat sales in 2013, its closest competitor owned only 6%. Then the NEST thermostat came along. It wasn't created from within the research labs at industry leaders such as Honeywell, Carrier, Trane, or Johnson Controls, but by two former Apple engineers. At first, Honeywell didn't respond to this new start-up company. Its classic "round" thermostat was untouchable – so Honeywell thought. By early 2017, Nest was nipping at Honeywell's heels for top spot in smart thermostat sales.

Nest is not the exception, but the rule these days. Amazon wasn't the next generation makeover that arose from within the retail industry. Airbnb wasn't started by the lodging industry. Uber and Lyft weren't new services launched from within the taxi or transportation industry. iTunes didn't come from the music industry just as Netflix wasn't the brainchild of an innovative TV or movie industry team. The list goes on and on.

It's not just executives and owners who need to look beyond what is in plain sight. Every worker from the cashier and bank teller to the attorney, accountant, and physician must anticipate and aggressively respond to the shift.

An HVAC technician is one of today's most in-demand jobs today. He might think his job is safe from foreign competition and cheap labor in Mexico; that only workers that manufacture the equipment he installs are at risk for automation. He doesn't make the connection that 3D printing, robots, drones, and autonomous vehicles could derail his career too. Despite above average demand today, the HVAC technician carries a 65% probability of automation by 2030.[11]

The auto body repair shop owner dismisses how driver-assisted technologies are projected to cut auto accidents by 50 to 90%. The internal combustion engine's heyday is long gone. What happens when the bread-and-butter oil change or 30,000 mile check-up is history? With fewer accidents and repairs, automobile related businesses have less work, require fewer helpers, purchase fewer supplies, and ultimately make less money. The trickledown effect of disruptive technologies is exponential. These technologies are the rocket fuel for the accelerating change that is making mincemeat out of tradition and convention. Time-tested business models are crumbling. Consumer markets are experiencing unprecedented flux, turmoil, and evolution.

Here's the bottom line: In a world connected by the Internet and globalization, everything we do is interdependent, and seemingly unrelated events have far-reaching effects. Exponential change requires organizations to stop hiring more window cleaners while watching their buildings burn. Individuals need to recognize that more than one-third of all jobs that exist today may be eliminated soon, and an even greater number of jobs will be significantly automated.

Embracing the scope and impact of exponential change is difficult even for those of us who experience and explore it every day. While participating in a recent summit on technology, I heard a brilliant question that pretty much sums up what every executive and business owner must ask himself:

What outsider like Uber, Airbnb, Apple, or Netflix might erupt out of nowhere to transform my business or industry? What technological disruptors such as artificial intelligence, robotics, 3D printing, and sensors might bankrupt my business in the next 2 years?

Employees should be asking:

What technological disruptors might replace my job and the work I do within 5 to 10 years? What technology might digitize my work and eliminate my job?

As long as change is linear, incremental, and occurs over decades, companies and people can resist and even weather technological disruption no worse for the wear. But with the intensity and velocity of change accelerating, businesses, institutions, and individuals are poorly prepared and ill-equipped to deal with massive transformative disruption or exponential change.

This disruption has created an environment that the military calls VUCA – Volatile, Uncertain, Complex, and Ambiguous. VUCA gives you the feeling you are standing in the middle of a category 5 hurricane that crosses the path of an F-5 tornado while the ground collapses beneath you due to a 10.0 earthquake. A catchall for VUCA might be "It's crazy out there."[12] It isn't uncommon to read about companies and leaders who are on the top of the world one day and hanging on for dear life the next.[13] To add to the uncertainty, life on the other side of exponential change is always radically different than the one left behind.

This uncertainty and volatility spur some people to want to run for the hills. Others choose to just duck and hide. Like Dorothy in search of the Wizard of Oz, we're not in Kansas anymore, Toto! There is no wizard behind the curtain to whisk VUCA away. To make change work, organizations and individuals must SHIFT how they think, prepare, work, and even play.

Now take a deep breath, slowly exhale, and let's begin the journey.

Is There an Elephant in Your Executive Office?

This "telephone" has too many shortcomings to be seriously considered as a means of communication. The device is inherently of no value to us.

Western Union internal memo, 1876.

Everything that can be invented has been invented.

Charles H. Duell, Commissioner, U.S. Office of Patents, 1899

The development of the automobile has been so remarkable that we do not expect any further improvements in the future.

German car manufacturer, 1914

There is a world market for about five computers.

Thomas Watson, founder and chairman of IBM, 1943

Television won't be able to hold on to any market it captures after the first six months. People will soon get tired of staring at a plywood box every night.

Darryl Zanuck, executive at 20th Century Fox,

1946

There is no reason anyone would want a computer in their home.

Ken Olsen, founder of Digital Equipment

Corporation, 1977

Apple is already dead.

Nathan Myhrvold, former Microsoft CTO, 1997

I wish we had moved faster.

Mike Duke, former Walmart CEO, 2017

[We] didn't anticipate how much Amazon would threaten the retail industry.

Warren Buffett, Berkshire Hathaway CEO, 2017

SHIFT

Shift Happens Fast

Future shock is the shattering stress and disorientation that we induce in individuals by subjecting them to too much change in too short a time.

Alvin Toffler[14]

By the time you finish reading this list (about 60 seconds), here are just a few things that changed around the world and inside our bodies!

- » There were 5 earthquakes around the world
- » Lightning struck the earth 6000 times
- » 3 violent crimes took place in the US
- » 8 people were injured in a car accident
- » 2638 mobile phones were sold
- » 24,733 apps downloaded from Apple Store
- » People checked their phones 5.5 million times
- » 3,437,500 videos viewed on YouTube
- » 700,000 people logged into Facebook
- » 250 babies were born
- » 144 people moved to a new home

» 116 people got married

» 107 people died

» 30,000 skin cells were shed

» 6 million chemical reactions took place inside every single cell in your body

» 120 million new red blood cells were created

» 600 million bits of visual information were received and sent to your brain

» 86 billion electrical signals were sent out by your brain

» 4 people applied at Google

» 36 people were interviewed at Amazon

» 7 Baby Boomers turned 60 years old

» 8 Millennials turned 30 years old

Mark Zuckerberg made $50,925! Bill Gates made $40,509! And Jeff Bezos made $39,007! (Source: CNBC, May 2016)

It's just mindboggling when you think about how our world and lives change every 60 seconds. What is more remarkable is that most of it happens without us noticing. But it's not nearly as crazy as when you multiply that 1 minute by 60 and ponder how much we change every hour. Multiply again by 24 hours and you get an even better picture of how our world changes each and every day. Then multiply again by 365 days and WOW! The world has changed more in the last year than it did in a lifetime for many of our ancestors.

Welcome to the era of exponential and accelerating change and all the good, bad, and different things that it brings.

It's Really Different This Time

DISRUPTIVE TECHNOLOGY AND innovation have a way of stirring the pot. Large shifts in technology, automation, and connectivity, as we're experiencing today, disrupt how we govern, live, work, and play. They bring large-scale change to our geopolitics and socio-economic structures and even the type of work people do.

During such upheavals, it's not uncommon for many of us to feel as if we are walking face-forward, naked and barefoot, through a storm of shattered glass. As in every previous industrial disruption, the winners of the previous era want to hold onto their success and the security of the past.[15] Anxiety and fear permeates the air. People romanticize about yesterday and rationalize away the enormity of change that surrounds them today.

Resistance to such change has a long-storied history. Let's start out with this simple quiz.

What's the first thing that comes to mind when asked these questions:

1. What technology makes men lazy?

2. What technology breaks up home life?

If you answered "social media" or the "Internet," you have a lot of company. Millions of people seem to be freaking out these days about these "nuisances" and "distractions." But life has a funny way of repeating itself.

These same questions were asked ninety years ago. Of course, that was years before anyone even thought about the Internet or social media. Back then the conversation focused on a new life-disrupting technology called the "telephone." Yes, you read that correctly. Ninety years ago, a national debate raged about how the telephone was the Devil's work. It was 1926 and the Knights of Columbus Adult Education Committee proposed that its group meetings discuss the impact of the telephone as well as "radio's impact on morality."[16]Sound familiar? Of course, it does.

Disruptive innovations like the telephone have been part of our lives since the beginning of mankind. The invention of the wheel transformed how people and goods moved. You might even imagine a time way back when a young innovative caveman introduced the wheel. I'm confident he wouldn't have to go far to hear the naysayers complain "the wheel will make men lazy" or, "that's not the way we do things around here" or, "people will get hurt." Disruption has happened before … and it will happen again.

The printing press set off an information revolution. The telegraph was replaced by the radio, then the television, and now the Internet. Whenever the status quo is threatened, people from all walks of life seem to put aside their differences and band together to resist. It's just a fact of life that when faced with disruption, it's easier to stick to familiar ways.

In the early part of the 20th century, pundits scoffed that automobiles and tractors would make horses irrelevant. Why? Because using horses for transportation and to assist manual labor was the status quo. It was also the bread-and-butter of many businesses and livelihood for many people. The combustion engine ended all that and many people lost their jobs and businesses closed when demand disappeared. The U.S. equine population meanwhile declined over 88%, taking with it businesses and jobs. Within 60 years, engine-driven vehicles clogged the roadways and disrupted business models, society, government, and even entire industries. Now it's the combustion engine itself that is ready to be sent out to pasture as automobile manufacturers race toward producing only electric or hybrid vehicles.

And just about 50 years before the engine-driven vehicle, the Luddites protested the introduction of spinning frames and power looms by smashing all of those job-killing machines. It wasn't long afterward that many of them were without jobs too while neighbors and relatives found better work in a new economy.

As history tends to repeat itself, complacency and hubris is again blinding many organizations and individuals to the writing on the wall. Jobs that once were a pathway to a middle-class lifestyle and a lifetime of employment are being eliminated. The discharged workers are unprepared to fill the new more specialized and skilled jobs being created. Executives and business owners view the future through a rear-view mirror and arrogantly dismiss the vulnerability of their products, services, and even business models. The status quo seems like the safe bet. It often is not.

If something seems really different this time, it isn't your imagination. The competition and the commitment to survive feel more intense because they are.

Conventional economic stimulators, employment models, and business strategies aren't working like they used to. Never have the peaks of success and valleys of failure erupted and fallen so quickly. According to A.T. Kearney's Turbulence Index, our operating environment is probably twice as volatile as it was 10 years ago.[17] This acceleration of change has become a disruptor in its own right.

Ray Kurzweil may sum it up best in his book, *The Age of Spiritual Machines: When Computers Exceed Human Intelligence.*

We're entering an age of acceleration. The models underlying society at every level, which are largely based on a linear model of change, are going to have to be redefined. Because of the explosive power of exponential growth, the 21st century will be equivalent to 20,000 years of progress at today's rate of progress; organizations have to be able to redefine themselves at a faster and faster pace.

Experts at McKinsey & Company[18] agree:

Compared with the Industrial Revolution, we estimate that change is happening ten times faster and at 300 times the scale, or roughly 3,000 times the impact. Although we all know that these disruptions are happening, most of us fail to comprehend their full magnitude and the second- and third-order effects that will result.

The Internet of Things (IoT) is now connecting everything. Every person has limitless access to infinite possibilities at the click of a key or the swipe of a screen. All this occurs in a world that seems to be infused with a continuous dose of volatility, uncertainty, complexity, and ambiguity. What makes it even more challenging is that all these forces work collectively to create a historic and disruptive tug of war between opportunity and chaos.

KEY POINTS

» Disruptive technology has been part of lives since the beginning of mankind. This time it is really different.

» The 21st century will be equivalent to 20,000 years of progress at today's rate of change.

» Change is happening 10 times faster and 300 times the scale with 3,000 times the impact compared to the Industrial Revolution.

VUCA is Our Kryptonite

MAKING SENSE OF CHANGE is nothing new; human nature seems to instill a love-hate relationship with it. But increasing volatility and an unprecedented uptick in the pace of change seems to be making the most resilient people on the planet a bit anxious.

It's no wonder so many people yearn for the good old days, when one could count on the certainty and predictability of simple choices—do A, then B happens. Economists and bureaucrats quelled public discomfort by adjusting policies based on the predictability of the "cycle." Good times were followed by bad times, which were followed by good times again, which were followed by ... well, you get the picture. Persistence and steadfastness were all that mattered. If you waited out the downturn, good times returned again and things went back to normal.

Unfortunately, exponential change doesn't follow the rules of linear growth and history. It lures many companies, their managers, and workers into a state of complacency. Persistence turns into stubbornness. Attempts to outrace and outlast the past only dig a deeper and inescapable hole for even iconic brands and companies. They ignore Albert Einstein's wise advice: "Doing the same thing over and over and expecting different results is the definition of insanity."

The U.S. military recognized something was different in the early 1990s. While the rest of the world watched the fall of the Berlin Wall, they saw a new world order. It shifted its strategy and even coined a funny sounding acronym to deal with what they anticipated would be a state of continuous disruption. They called it VUCA. Independently, each word describes an element of change that instills anxiety and agitation. As tempting as it is, you just can't beat around the bush this time. VUCA is the ultimate challenge leaders (and individuals) face today. It's not government regulations, climate change, or immigration. It's not Congress or ISIS or North Korea. It's not technology or globalization. It's not social media or education. It is four elements of change working collaboratively and synergistically, antagonistically and asynchronously. And not a single one acts in a vacuum.

The convergence of **V**olatility, **U**ncertainty, **C**omplexity, and **A**mbiguity demands a response that ignites passion and instills meaning and purpose, not fear. Executives of all organizations must change their approach toward leadership. Human Resources professionals must revamp people and workforce management. Individuals must retool their career paths and lifestyles.

KEY POINTS

Volatility is turbulence; it's the nature, speed, volume, and magnitude of change. We might have the knowledge and even be able to predict the outcome…but with volatility, you may not have the time to plan or react. The issue with volatility is simply the rate of change, one that is accelerating beyond our ability to keep up.

Uncertainty relates to the lack of predictability of issues and events. Information about the past and present are less and less useful in anticipating the future. Uncertainty makes forecasting difficult and decision-making challenging. We might know quite a bit about the situation but we're unsure what to do next.

Complexity represents the difficult-to-understand causes and mitigating factors involved in a problem brought about in an increasingly intertwined world. Complexity requires the need to make multiple key decisions that can impact and influence our options and outcomes. Each decision influences another in unintentional and unanticipated ways. Complexity clouds our judgment.

Ambiguity represents the world of unknown unknowns, the haziness of reality and the mixed meanings of similar-but-different conditions that can lead to different outcomes. It makes it difficult to grasp the meaning of fast moving, unclear, and complex events.

WELCOME TO A WORLD
OF EXPONENTIAL CHANGE

B OB JOHANSEN, AN esteemed researcher at the Institute for the Future, offers another perspective on why living with VUCA is so different. He believes we are moving "from a world of problems to a world of continuous dilemmas."[19]

Dilemmas differ from problems in significant ways. Specifically, problems can be solved by a single expert or a small specialized team. They demand speed, analysis, and elimination of uncertainty. Experience and education matter. In fact, experience and education could be enough to qualify you as the go-to person, the subject matter expert, in a world of just problems. Living in a world of dilemmas, it's a whole new ballgame.

Dilemmas can't be solved; they can be managed. That's because dilemmas are messy, complicated, conflict-filled, and span many disciplines. Even when solutions seem possible, volatility and complexity inject uncertainty and ambiguity which often present a choice among multiple undesirable and/or unpredictable options. Traditional problem solvers try to "get their head around it" to craft a definitive solution. They attempt to over-simplify complicated and complex problems. They struggle living in a world of unknown unknowns. Managing dilemmas require a different orientation, an innovative mindset, an analytical decision process, and a set of diverse skills. "Dilemma managers" see possibilities, alternatives, and opportunity.

Of course, it is tempting for business, and more so for individuals, to dismiss VUCA. The military is concerned with sovereign instability, wars, and terrorism, right? Let the military deal with VUCA and keep the rest of us out of it. That mindset might have worked in the past but it is completely and utterly useless today.

For management, living the future vicariously through the past is not only a dead-end; it's an end-of-life strategy. Look no further than Kodak. (Speaking of change ... my apologies to the young Millennials and Generation Z who might be reading and don't remember Kodak!)

Ed McNierney, who ran digital strategy at Kodak, blames complacency and hubris on the implosion of one of America's most famous brands. He notes "that bringing the dead weight of your legacy from your past into the future can be detrimental to the business." He should know, since Kodak peaked in 1996 with a $28 billion market cap and 140,000 employees. Fourteen years later ... it was bankrupt and out of business.

Unbelievably, Kodak invented the digital camera twenty years earlier but refused to put its name on it. Despite being the household name in the photo-taking business, they missed out on a boom that has seen the number of photos taken spike from 57 billion in 1990 to over 1.5 trillion today[20] ... and climb exponentially higher each year! Kodak literally held the keys to the future but lost them under all the paper and chemicals they sold for film development. They forgot what business they were really in: preserving memories.

Ironically, in the same year that Kodak disappeared, Facebook acquired a little-known start-up company in the digital imagery business called Instagram for 1 billion dollars. Instagram had only 13 employees.[21] By early 2017, more than 40 billion photos and videos have been uploaded and nearly 100 million are shared daily. Instagram is expected to generate $5 billion in 2018.

Corporate miscalculations like Kodak won't end anytime soon. We will experience a lot more Kodak moments in the very near future. Such is life in the world of exponential change.

Here's another sign of how quickly things change. Life expectancy of companies on the S&P (and other stock exchanges) is tumbling. An entire generation, and maybe two, have no memory of corporate giants like Bethlehem Steel, Digital Equipment, and RCA. More recently, most of us witnessed the rise and fall of Sears, Compaq, Blockbuster, Blackberry, Circuit City, AOL, and Yahoo.

Change is not new. It has plagued much of humanity from day one. Heraclitus, a Greek philosopher, was even quoted as saying "change is the only constant in life." Nevertheless, the velocity of change today is certainly something no man has ever experienced.

SPEAKING ABOUT VOLATILITY

If you want a real wake-up call on how fast things change, hand anyone under 20 years old a floppy disc and ask them if they've ever used one. If they recognize it at all, they will likely refer to it as a 3D printed object of the save icon located on most of our computers.

According to Yale Entrepreneurial Institute's Executive-in-Residence Richard Foster, the average lifespan of an S&P dropped from 67 years in the 1920s to 15 years today. More organizations and businesses are losing their edge and will become waste products of disruptive innovation. On average an S&P company is being replaced every two weeks.[22] In 10 years, it's predicted that 40% of the Fortune 500 companies will no longer exist.[23]

"The promises of science fiction are quickly becoming workday realities."[24] Those are the words of Andrew McAfee and Erik Brynjolfsson, the brilliant research scientists at the forefront of helping us understand the future. And those realities have huge implications for individuals too; especially the millions of them holding low-skill, low-wage jobs.

The U.S. Council of Economic Advisers estimates that 83% of jobs paying less than $20 per hour can be automated. Former McDonald's USA CEO goes even further: "It's cheaper to buy a $35,000 robotic arm than it is to hire an employee who is inefficient making $15 an hour bagging french fries."[25] And as the cost of robotics falls and labor costs rise, more low-skill/low-pay jobs will be lost.

Everything from individual tasks to entire careers is being disrupted. A landmark study by Carl Benedikt Frey and Michael Osborne predicts the automation of nearly half of U.S. jobs.[26] Nine of the top ten most in-demand jobs of 2012 did not exist in 2003.[27] Even the C-Suite is vulnerable![28] Since artificial intelligence is already used for predictive modeling and data analysis, it isn't difficult to imagine how the visioning role of the CEO could be next.

The reality is, VUCA will impact the lives of every human being living on the planet today. It will change how we work and play, where we live, how we move from place to place, and even how we will be governed. The temptation to preserve the status quo is irresistible but life during and after VUCA calls for an open mind, a positive attitude, innovative thinking, and new or advanced skills.

So, once we can agree that VUCA is here to stay and will touch the lives of every single person and impact every organization sooner rather than later, we can begin to approach finding viable solutions.

Making VUCA Work for You

Wherever you turn these days, people are arguing whether the glass is half empty or half full. Depending on the conversation, our world is either headed toward cataclysmic destruction or an age of unprecedented abundance.

At its core, VUCA infuses unpredictability into every decision. Failure, however, is neither inevitable nor a foregone conclusion. VUCA just defines the state of the environment. Some people are overwhelmed with stress and anxiety and tormented by a sense of helplessness. Others are emboldened, inspired, and energized by a future exploding with infinite opportunity. The decision to succumb to the volatility, uncertainty, complexity, and/or ambiguity of VUCA is just a choice—a bad one in my opinion, but a choice, nonetheless.

Fortunately, every person and every organization has viable options. No one is handing out get-out-of-jail-free cards to escape VUCA, but with vision, strategy, and commitment, VUCA can be your ally just as easily as it can be your Kryptonite. (We'll talk more about that in just a few pages.)

KEY POINTS

» We are moving from a world of problems to a world of nonstop dilemmas.

» The promises of science fiction are quickly becoming workday realities.

» VUCA will impact the lives of every human being on this planet.

QUESTIONS

» What seems odd in my competitive landscape?

» What new patterns are emerging?

» Do I need to change the way I respond to problems?

» Am I denying things that don't fit my view of the world?

WHY EXPONENTIAL CHANGE IS DIFFERENT

IT'S EASY FOR "MATURE" and "experienced" leaders and workers to dismiss the power of VUCA. It's true they have fought, adapted, persevered and thrived through change in the past. Success instills a natural sense of confidence. In fact, many succeeded by just "sticking to the plan." Why not just stay the course and do it again?

As I mentioned earlier, change this time is not just an evolutionary event that makes things different from the past. The rate of such change is accelerating and it is doing so exponentially. And exponential change is disruptive. Let's take a quick look at history. It might be easier to grasp how today's disruptive change is so different from anything in the past.

The Agrarian age lasted about 8,000 years until it was disrupted by the Industrial Revolution. The time lapse from the Industrial Revolution (mid-19th century) to the Computer Age (1960s) was just about one century. But it only took 40 years until we experienced the Information Age. And now in about half that time we are entering the Cyber-Mental era, when humans and robots function collaboratively and interdependently. A more generic title might be the Human-Machine era. Technology has tipped the scale to a time when technology doesn't just make humans more productive, but humans and technology will interact.

While this sounds crazy, awkward to many of us, robots will be able to read our minds![29] It is well within the realm of reality that within a few years we might even drive a car or fly a plane with our thoughts alone. But I'm getting ahead of myself.

Let me get back to describing the impact of exponential change. One of the best visualizations to demonstrate how exponential change works was inspired by Tony Lloyd, CEO of *CultureShift* and author of *VUCA: Leadership Stories of Volatility, Uncertainty, Complexity and Ambiguity.*

You've been offered a job to drive one hour away, pick up one penny, and drive back. The next day, you are to drive to the same place, return the penny, and be given double that amount or two pennies. You are to continue in this manner for 30 days, each day doubling your accumulated pennies. You are given the option to collect a check for $1,000,000 right now or wait until the end of the month and keep the pennies.

Which would you choose? Most of us would probably choose the flat fee of $1,000,000. But Marty, the math whiz, chooses to keep the pennies. On day 10, a third of the way through the month, Marty has only accumulated $5.12. On day 20, he's still only got $5,242.88 to show for his efforts. And on day 25, he picks up $167,772.16 worth of pennies. That's a lot of pennies, but he's still only 17% along the way to $1,000,000.

So, he's given the option once again to give up all those pennies and pick up a $1,000,000 check instead. But Marty is nothing if not stubborn, and he says he'll stick with the pennies. We shake our heads. The poor guy just made a big mistake. Or did he? Things are about to get interesting!

On day 28, Marty picks up $1,342,177.28. On day 29, it's

$2,624,354.56. And on day 30, as we stand there with our measly $1,000,000 checks, he walks away with $5,368,709.12 worth of pennies. It's little consolation to us that Marty's going to be spending the next several weeks of his life rolling pennies. We just made a really bad deal and missed an enormous opportunity because we didn't understand the power of exponential change.

Still not convinced? Here's the calculation!

Day 1: $.01	Day 16: $327.68
Day 2: $.02	Day 17: $655.36
Day 3: $.04	Day 18: $1,310.72
Day 4: $.08	Day 19: $2,621.44
Day 5: $.16	Day 20: $5,242.88
Day 6: $.32	Day 21: $10,485.76
Day 7: $.64	Day 22: $20,971.52
Day 8: $1.28	Day 23: $41,943.04
Day 9: $2.56	Day 24: $83,886.08
Day 10: $5.12	Day 25: $167,772.16
Day 11: $10.24	Day 26: $335,544.32
Day 12: $20.48	Day 27: $671,088.64
Day 13: $40.96	Day 28: $1,342,177.28
Day 14: $81.92	Day 29: $2,684,354.56
Day 15: $163.84	Day 30: $5,368,709.12

For 26 days, it looks as if not much is happening. But on day 27, a miracle occurs and the power of change erupts. That's the world we live in. Exponential change starts innocently enough but before you know it, it erupts and changes everything! It explains why Kodak along with countless other businesses ignored the deceptive nature of early stage exponential growth and then couldn't recover once the shift occurred.

Here are a few more examples that we accept as ambient and incidental noise but immensely impact each and every one of our lives.

Imagine two average adults about 5 feet 8 inches tall standing back to back. From shoulder to shoulder their width measures 29 inches and chest to chest, the distance is 60 inches. Now insert them in a heavy metal case, load it up so it weighs about 1 ton and you have the basic specifications of the world's first commercial hard drive in 1956. The storage capacity of this drive was a whopping 5 MB, the equivalent of one mp3 audio file or three high-resolution photos you took using your smartphone. The cost: $50,000. That's $10,000/MB or about $15,000 per photo.

Had technology crept along incrementally, and not exponentially, the hard drive resting in your palm inside your 16GB smartphone today would cost $160 million and weigh 3200 tons. Fortunately, that's not the case. We don't have to drag around thousands of those 1-ton hard drives to power our Fitbits and mobile devices. Today's hard drive can almost fit on your finger tip and store 16 terabytes of data —the equivalent to 86,000,000 pages of Word documents, 200,000 songs, 17,000 hours of music, 10,240 two-hour movies, or 310,000 pictures for the low, low price of less than $0.00003/MB.

Now imagine that same amount of change taking place every day! Yes, you read that correctly. Imagine the experience of 60 years of change compressed into 24 hours. That, my friends, is what is happening almost every day. You are not imagining that change is faster or more disruptive, because it is. The future is not coming. It is here.

Another example of change, although a bit less dramatic, is the Osborne Executive introduced in 1981. It was one of the first portable business computers. Its cost was $2,500, weighed about 28 pounds, and included 124 KB of memory. Let's fast forward to 2007 when the iPhone was introduced. It cost $500, weighed 0.28 pounds, was 150 X faster, and had 100,000 times more memory. More of us are familiar with GPS (Global Positioning System). The first commercial GPS receiver introduced in 1981 weighed 53 pounds and cost $119,900. The single chip GPS receiver included in smartphones today weighs a few grams and costs under $5.

Moore's Law has become the poster-child for change. It was the prediction in 1975 by Intel co-founder Gordon Moore that the number of transistors in a dense integrated circuit would double approximately every two years, while the price would remain constant. What many people ignored is that along with more transistors per microprocessor, the processing speed (clock speed) would also increase exponentially.

Today, the Chinese supercomputer Tianhe-2 can perform 33.86 petaflops per second. A petaflop is a quadrillion calculations. How fast is that? Well, it has been estimated by Casey Research[30] that to equal the processing power of the human brain requires 55 petaflops per second. Given the continuous, exponential rise of computer processing power, it won't take long for a computer to catch up. In May, 2015, Katja Grace and Paul Christiano calculated "it should take seven to fourteen years for a computer which costs $100/hour to be competitive with the human brain."

In other words, as early as 2022, a business will be able to rent computer processing power equal to the human brain for $100/hour.[31]

As crazy as that seems, genome sequencing is leaving Moore's Law in the dust. The Human Genome Project completed in 2003 took 13 years to complete and cost $2.7 billion. Because of the introduction of high throughput machines, the cost of sequencing the human genome is falling five times faster than the cost of computing. Today, it takes less than three days and costs less than $1,000 to sequence your DNA.

What's next? Let's return to my example of the hard drive for a minute. Remember how it took 60 years to reduce the size of the hard drive from the size of a small closest to one that fits on your fingertip? With the advent of quantum computing, the speed of computing will increase 100 million times. I'm not kidding or exaggerating. Quantum computing has the capability of figuring out complex algorithms at 100,000,000 times the speed of a traditional computer chip.[32] What that means is that what took 60 years to evolve in the past might be compressed into a day or even minutes or seconds.

Buckle up. The SHIFT will hit everyone's plan.

KEY POINTS

» History has produced 4 labor markets. We are transitioning to the 5th.

» The power of exponential change is staggering.

» You are not imagining that change is more disruptive or occurring faster.

QUESTIONS:

» What recent events indicate that "sticking to my plan" isn't such a good idea?

» How is the change I'm seeing today different than what I experienced 10 or 20 years ago?

» Who can help me understand what is happening?

» What happens when quantum computing goes live and the speed of processing information increase 100 million times overnight?

How Close Is the Shift?

So that leaves us with an obvious question: How soon do we need to be worried that our jobs, our work, and our way of life will be significantly disrupted?

As I mentioned earlier, it's easy to blow off and even laugh at signs of incremental change. It's only human nature that past success instills a sense of complacency and even justifiable arrogance. But let's take a look how easily the pedestal can be knocked out from under us and how powerful the downdraft can be. Consider the self-driving car.

For sure, the autonomous vehicle will impact the auto manufacturers and their workers. Supply chains will be disrupted. It will affect the workers who build, maintain, and service these cars too. And what about taxi, bus, and truck drivers? What will happen to them?

Disruption has a very large blast zone that inflicts extensive collateral damage far down the supply chain. (It also creates enormous opportunity depending upon your viewpoint and mindset.) In its recent annual report filing with the SEC, Allstate Corporation, one the largest automobile insurance companies in the U.S., stated:

Other potential technological changes, such as driverless cars or technologies that facilitate ride or home sharing could disrupt the demand for our products from current customers, create coverage issues or impact the frequency or severity of losses, and we may not be able to respond effectively. [33]

> **FOR THE RECORD**
>
> A "TIPPING POINT" IS DEFINED AS THE MOMENT OF CRITICAL MASS, THE THRESHOLD, THE BOILING POINT.

Today, car crashes have an enormous impact on the U.S. economy. With driverless cars, accident rates are expected to plummet, especially serious ones. With more electric cars, gas sales will go down which means less tax revenues for government. Revenues from traffic violations will dive. With more shared vehicles, parking and toll revenue will drop too. How will federal, state, and local governments adapt to this changing world? Are they even thinking about it or do elected officials and bureaucrats feel they can legislate disruption away?

Closer to home, how imminent is your tipping point? You have permission to take a deep breath and puff your chest out one last time, savoring all you have accomplished. But it's time to put a pin in it and stick the trophies and awards on the shelf. The tipping point or "SHIFT" for many jobs and businesses is knocking, if it hasn't already swung past you.

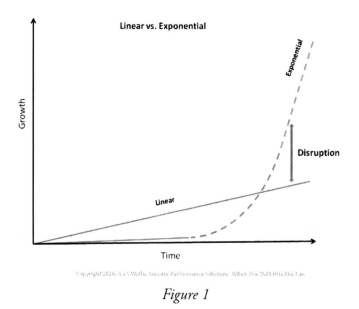

Figure 1

Once the exponential growth curve crosses the linear and incremental growth path of an existing organization or industry, past success is history and demand for those products, services, or skills evaporates. Welcome to the disruption zone. It's when the shift hits your plan that it's difficult if not impossible to recover.

Exponential change, whether driven by 3D printing, data analytics, robotics, autonomous vehicles, artificial intelligence, or renewable energy, has far-reaching consequences. These technologies in fact were just a few examples of imminent disruptors identified by many of the world's leading "movers and shakers" at a recent World Economic Forum in Davos, Switzerland.

Likelihood of Tipping Points to Occur by 2025[33]	%
10% of people wearing clothes connected to the Internet	91.2
90% of people having unlimited and free storage	91.0
1 trillion sensors connected to the Internet	89.2
The 1st robotic pharmacist in the US	86.5
The 1st 3-D printed car in production	84.1
The 1st implantable mobile phone available commercially	81.7
Driverless cars make up 10% of all cars on US roads	78.2
The 1st transplant of a 3D-printed liver	76.4
The 1st city with more than 50,000 people and no traffic lights	63.7

This partial listing of tipping points and likelihood of mass adoption was revealed in a survey conducted by the Global Agenda Council on the Future of Software & Society in March 2015.[35] It asked 800+ executives when they thought specific technologic shifts would hit mainstream society. Next is another chart indicating when each tipping point is expected to occur. Quite a few of them will occur much sooner than 2027.

WHEN SHIFT MAY HIT YOUR PLAN

2018	2021	2022	2023	2024	2025	2026	2027
Storage for all	Robot and services	The Internet of and for Things	Implantable Technologies	Ubiquitous Computing	3D Printing and Consumer Products	Driverless Cars	Bitcoin and the Blockchain
		Wearable Internet	Big Data for Decisions	3D Printing and Human Health	AI and White Collar Jobs	AI and Decision Making	
		3D Printing and Manufacturing	Vision as the New Interface	The Connected Home	The Sharing Economy	Smart Cities	
			Our Digital Presence				
			Supercomputer in Your Pocket				

Source: http://www3.weforum.org/docs/WEF_GAC15_
Technological_Tipping_Points_report_2015.pdf

While the tipping point for many of these changes are imminent, many companies and careers today seem to be stuck in those first "25 days of exponential change" when linear growth and incremental change is still on their side. But time is running out and the shift is nipping at their heels. New competition doesn't seem to be just a few moves ahead but playing another game entirely.

Ask almost anyone what United Parcel Service does and you'll probably hear, "deliver packages." They would be right—sort of. It is true that UPS delivers more than 19 million packages daily to nearly 9 million customers in 200 countries. But did you know UPS recently announced that it had created a fully distributed manufacturing platform, connecting 60 of The UPS Stores, each with mid-level 3D printers, onto an advanced production platform built and run by parts manufacturer, Fast Radius. You can call UPS and 3D print a part you need and pick it up in just a few hours. Need 5,000 "widgets" for a rush order? UPS and others will be able to do that too with large-scale 3D printing going mainstream and the cost of 3D printers falling precipitously.

It doesn't stop there. Remember how desktop publishing disrupted the printing industry in the 1990s—when anyone with a computer and minimal skills could design and print marketing materials? A funny thing happened to me when I was researching the UPS-Fast Radius collaboration. I discovered a young man with a dozen 3D printers in his basement producing more than 10,000 fidget spinners for sale. Manufacturing is on the cusp of a massive disruption, unlike anything it's seen in 200 hundred years. When all it takes is a handful of 3D printers to mass produce parts for almost anything, the biggest threat might not be cheap products from a developing country but quality products manufactured in the basement of an entrepreneur. But why stop there? What's stopping Amazon from purchasing a manufacturer of large-scale 3D printers and becoming a one-stop-shop supply chain for just about anything?

As you just learned (hopefully), past success no longer entitles you to a future legacy, especially when a new competitor, product, or service can seem to appear spontaneously out of nowhere and rock your world. If you're not looking and listening, you'll miss the shift and be swallowed up by the speed and disruption of exponential change.

The tales of Kodak-like failures and demises have become legendary. Thanks to this exponential accelerating rate of change, they will occur regularly with greater frequency.

How Susceptible is Your Job to Automation?[36]

Telemarketer	99%
Tax Preparer	99%
Insurance Underwriter	99%
Loan Officers	98%
Bank Tellers	98%
Legal Secretaries	98%
Real Estate Brokers	97%
Dental and Ophthalmic Lab Techs	97%
Cooks	96%
Administrative Assistants	96%
Paralegals	94%
Welders	94%
Waiters and Waitresses	94%
Accountants and Auditors	94%
Retail Salesperson	92%
Insurance Sales Agents	92%
Medical Records and Health Information Technicians	91%
Automotive Body and Related Repairers	91%
Roofers	90%
Human Resources Assistants	90%

How Susceptible is Your Job to Automation?[37]

Recreational Therapists	0.2%
First-Line Supervisors of Mechanics, Installers, and Repairers	0.3%
Emergency Management Directors	0.3%
Mental Health and Substance Abuse Social Workers	0.3%
Audiologists	0.3%
Occupational Therapists	0.3%
Oral and Maxillofacial Surgeons	0.3%
Lodging Managers	0.4%
Sales Engineers	0.4%
Physicians and Surgeons	0.4%
Dentists	0.4%
Elementary School Teachers	0.4%
Human Resources Managers	0.5%
Computer Systems Analysts	0.6%
Athletic Trainers	0.7%
Farm and Home Management Advisors	0.7%
Clergy	0.8%
Registered Nurses	0.9%
Mechanical Engineers	1%
Sales Managers	1%

For a listing of 702 occupations and The Future of Employment, go to http://www.oxfordmartin.ox.ac.uk/downloads/academic/The_Future_of_Employment.pdf

KEY POINTS

» Disruptive technology has a far reaching "blast" area.

» The tipping point for many technologies is closer than you think.

» Past success no longer entitles you to a future.

QUESTIONS:

» What tipping points should I be watching that might impact my business or career?

» How will my customers, vendors, and suppliers be impacted by disruptive technology?

» How likely is it that I will be caught in the downdraft of their change?

Business Gets an "F"

So how are organizations and their management responding? To date, the VUCA-readiness report card reveals a big fat, red "F."

In a recent PwC study, only 8% of senior executives were found to have the right skills to lead organization-wide transformations.[38] Thomas Friedman (*The World Is Flat*) observes that VUCA is taxing even the most able of leaders who may find their skills growing obsolete as quickly as their organizations change in this volatile, unpredictable landscape.[39]

To make matters worse, only 4 out of 10 organizations have a clear set of leadership indicators and over 50% of companies admit they lack succession plans.

It's also not enough to just hire leaders with potential or a proven track record. Leadership agility and the ability to improvise on the fly are now crucial skills if organizations are to succeed in this VUCA world. No one has ever run this VUCA track before. Selection and development must be focused on identifying and building leaders with critical thinking skills, the ability to innovate, a passion for continuing learning, resourcefulness, and adaptability.

High emotional intelligence is also a must in a VUCA world,

where stress and anxiety are endemic. It's equally important to manage the emotions of others, as well as your own. The ability to inspire others with both empathy and skill is essential. These requirements are a far cry from the more technical-specific skills and abilities leaders needed in the past to succeed.

Regrettably, most companies are doing a horrendous job of identifying and developing VUCA-ready talent—from the production floor to the board room. Management still seems to value looking in the rear-view mirror of past experience and degrees attained more than visioning forward.

DUCK-AND-HIDE WON'T WORK

Putting the right people in place is just the start. It is the right people who must create a new vision and strategy, tell the story, and have the wherewithal to execute it with a sense of direction and urgency.

Let me paint an absolutely crystal-clear picture about what I just said: If you or your management team are "working on it" or "are planning to discuss it at our next strategic retreat" or (my favorite excuse) "our industry is different," then your business model and business itself are very likely accidents just waiting to happen. Linear growth cannot fend off disruption. "Waiting for things to play out" or "keeping an eye on our competitors" is not a realistic or productive approach in a VUCA-world.

The first thing every executive must do is ask himself: Is the team of people who got us to where we are today capable enough to get us where we want to go? Loyalty goes a long way and, regrettably, it has become an elusive quality in today's instant-gratification marketplace. But it's also naïve to ignore that some people are not willing or able to make the changes needed. Every employee deserves the opportunity to grow and succeed. But no one is entitled to a paycheck, including the CEO, just because he or she has a history of success when VUCA is an existential threat.

It's equally as arrogant to think you are smart enough to wait-and-see then react swiftly to a tsunami of exponential change. VUCA waits for nothing and no one. It doesn't play favorites. It takes no mercy on small budgets and stretched thin resources. It doesn't play by the rules. It doesn't wait for an appointment on your calendar. At best, protecting the status quo provides a false sense of security. Ultimately it places your business on life support.

The need for significant transformation is now.

An Antidote for VUCA?

THERE'S AN OLD STORY that has made its rounds: To succeed, you don't need to outrun the bear, you just need to outrun your nearest competitor. The problem in a VUCA world is that your biggest competitor today may be invisible—not a known competitor from within your industry. It's just as likely to be a start-up company that threatens to disrupt an industry, challenge conventional business models, or democratize a service. It pops up out of nowhere, and seems to change everything almost overnight.

Failure to adapt or respond is often not due to a lack of opportunity. In a world that demands immediate gratification, organizations feel compelled to deliver fast results to shareholders. Many disruptive innovations like Kodak's digital camera never get to see the light of day even though the convergence of technology, fast changing consumer trends, and globalization creates unexpected and boundless new pathways and possibilities.

Winston Churchill once said, "A pessimist sees the difficulty in every opportunity; an optimist sees the opportunity in every difficulty." Here are today's optimists and opportunists. It is the 18-year-old entering college, the 25-year-old trying to launch his first business, the 45-year-old who leaves a rising career to spearhead a start-up, and the 65-year-old entrepreneur attempting to have one more "go-at-it." What drives them to see doors of opportunity when so many others see walls? They all share one thing in common —a mindset that says "our journey is only 1% complete."

Those words —"our journey is only 1% complete"—lie behind the success of Facebook. They are not just motivational words plastered on walls, but embody the internal motto at Facebook. They might and should demoralize any Gen X or Baby Boomer who sees the finish line within his grasp. For those who fear change and prefer to focus all their energy onto holding back the hands of time, "our journey is only 1% complete" can terrify and debilitate.

Facebook takes its motto seriously. You should too. It's a constant reminder that everyone is on a journey and in spite of the phenomenal success Facebook enjoys, it doesn't believe it has arrived yet. It doesn't even believe it's a quarter or half-way there. The message behind the motto even infiltrates the design of its headquarters—the office looks unfinished on purpose.

Facebook is not alone on this journey. Tom Ashbrook, host of NPR's OnPoint, in a recent interview exclaimed "Oh My God" when his guest Chris Lehane, Airbnb's Head of Global Policy and Communications, stated "What we see now in terms of disruption [referring to Airbnb, Facebook, Amazon, Google, Apple, Uber and a few others] are just the lemonade stands in front of what's to come."

The story doesn't end there. Another reminder at Facebook that continuous success isn't a destination, but a journey, is the last sign employees see each day exiting the workplace.

Facebook's headquarters used to belong to Sun Microsystems,

a onetime power-house of innovation that collapsed and was acquired by Oracle in 2009. When Facebook moved in, Zuckerberg made over the whole place, but he didn't change the sign out front; he just turned it around and put Facebook on the other side. Every time an employee leaves the Facebook campus he sees the Sun Microsystems sign; it's a constant reminder about what happens when you take your eye off the ball. It is Facebook founder and CEO Mark Zuckerberg's not-so-subtle message to his Facebook employees: We don't want to end up like Sun Microsystems.

The Facebook-Sun Microsystems sign is just one symbol that change does not even begin to describe what is happening in the world today. Learning to deal with "change" takes on a whole new meaning. It requires us to become comfortable with volatility and uncertainty, to navigate through complexity, to deal with ambiguity. Consequently, the skills that got many of us to our current level of success will be wholly inadequate to keep the momentum going. This is not a future vision of some distant threat or opportunity. It is reality today.

But before you reach the conclusion that I'm unleashing a wholesale dump on leadership, let me acknowledge that it's not that today's leaders are not smart or aware about what's going on. Most of them didn't get where they are today without many admirable attributes, qualities, and successes. The problem is that the speed of change is simply overwhelming many of them.[40]

VUCA readiness requires shedding old assumptions and acquiring new mindsets. It mandates organizations to take leadership development, succession planning, and talent management seriously. Behavioral change, rather than just acquiring more degrees, competencies, and skills, must be emphasized.[41] Emotional intelligence has become more important than general intelligence. To succeed going forward, business leaders must be transformative.

Of course, transformative change is, by its very nature, overwhelming. When overwhelmed by stressful circumstances, the higher order "executive" functions of our brains literally shut down. Our ability to function becomes impaired. That makes it easy to use VUCA as the rationale for poor performance and an excuse for failure. After all, you can't prepare for a VUCA world, right?[42]

Actually, you can. Fortunately, the power of exponential change can work for you too, not just against you. VUCA-savvy leaders embrace VUCA and seem to navigate through the disruption and complexity and come out ahead. How do they do this?

They "flip" the VUCA model. Bob Johansen calls this, VUCA Prime. He proposes that the best VUCA leaders are characterized by Vision, Understanding, Clarity, and Agility. HR and talent management professionals can use VUCA Prime as a blueprint for success in a VUCA world.[43]

What is VUCA Prime?

Vision mitigates volatility. Vision instills a powerful motivation to create a better future. The speed and turbulence of change won't go away but fear and anxiety do fade when your strategy is guided by a clear vision. With vision, you see past the small distractions so that you're able to stay focused on the bigger picture. Vision doesn't only benefit you but it helps you serve others better. It helps align your decisions with your values. But beware—a vision isn't just a statement or poster you hang on the wall. It's something you feel. Don't B.S. yourself or others. It won't work. For a vision to become possible, it must be realistic and you must be authentic.

Understanding defuses uncertainty. It sure seems like the only thing in life that is certain is that uncertainty will continue. But that doesn't mean moving forward requires that you take a blind leap into the unknown. There is a huge difference between change leading you and you dancing with it step by step. To be effective in a VUCA environment, leaders must learn to dance with change. Ask challenging questions. Teach and coach others. Accept and welcome feedback. Develop, build, and manage networks of teams.[44] Make sure you're open to and getting fresh perspective, no matter how outrageous the source or idea. (You'll read more about a tool called "info-sponging" later.) Understanding also requires that decisions are based less on tradition and anecdote and made with more data-driven evidence. (Evidence-based decisions are discussed in more detail in the chapter on People Analytics.) Recognize your limitations but don't let them cripple you.

Clarity helps simplify complexity. Articulate and communicate clearly. To reach clarity and make better decisions faster, make it a practice to seek different perspectives. Ask the question: What is the most effective way to meet the needs of the market, not the business? Be deliberate in your attempt to make sense of the chaos. Don't forget that communication is a two-way street and collaboration is a key. Actively observe and make sense of what you see. But don't dismiss perplexing and unusual answers. Set realistic expectations for yourself and communicate them to others. Strive for perfection and think of mistakes and failures as a resource you've already paid for. Accept that "permanent" fixes and solutions in a VUCA world have a short shelf-life.

Agility tames Ambiguity. A quick search for a description of agility on Google brings up 10,500,000 results in half a second. Here's my capsule version: the ability to see around corners, connect the dots, and respond quickly and effectively whenever the situation changes. Most organizations do pretty well at what they do today. It's what they need to be doing tomorrow that is missing. The same can be said about individuals too. Agility shifts the mindset from "I don't see how change will affect me or the organization" or "I don't see how I/we can do anything about it?" to "I know change is coming and this is what I'm/we're going to do to respond." Disruptions will happen but the element of surprise is lost when you anticipate the subtle changes and respond with agility.

KEY POINTS

» Disruptive technologies and innovation are disrupting how we live, work, play, and govern.

» VUCA changes everything. We used to live in a world of problems. Today we experience a world of dilemmas.

» Buckle up. SHIFT will hit everyone's plan.

» VUCA Prime gets individuals and organizations ready for prime time.

QUESTIONS EVERY EXECUTIVE, BUSINESS OWNER, AND WORKER MUST ASK *AND* ANSWER:

» How will change disrupt my job, career, or business in the next 2 to 5 years?

» How is technology disrupting my industry and what am I doing to ensure that my business does not get left behind?

» How will exponential technologies change the competition in our industry?

» How will exponential technologies impact our business model?

» Who are emerging competitors?

» How will technology help us win against traditional and new competitors?

» If the most prominent player in our industry did go away, what opportunities would it open up?

» Which of our key products or services are most vulnerable to disruption from an emerging product or service?

» What will our customers expect in the future?

» Will our current plans and strategies capitalize on opportunities and neutralize threats?

» How realistic are our time horizons?

» How does our ability to attract and retain talent measure up with our competitors?

» What are our weakest links in our ability to attract and retain top talent?

» How will we know when our current strategy, business plan, or career is on the verge of collapse?

» What feature can we create that's missing in someone else's product or service?

It's All in Your Head

When *Jurassic Park* owner, John Hammond promised nothing could go wrong when he wanted to have T-Rexes romp around an island, Dr. Malcom did not agree. "Life finds a way," chaos theory expert Malcolm said.

Life is complex. The only reliable prediction you can make is that it is unpredictable. Business, one part of this much larger ecosystem called life, is no exception. And yet many organizations and its managers persist in their belief that cause and effect is linear: If you increase base pay, employees will be more engaged, productivity will rise, turnover will fall, and everyone will live happy forever after.

Of course, few of us believe people management is quite this simple. Competitors dangle more money and benefits to entice your best workers to jump ship. The personal lives of workers create a steady stream of HR challenges too. Child care, elder care, illness, divorce, marriage, and pregnancy disrupt employee performance, attendance, and attrition. The list of possible variables is a very long list, yet these factors fail to take into consideration the impact on productivity and performance from uncontrollable environmental events ranging from inclement weather to terrorism. The bottom line is that being prepared for the future is more complex than ever before.

How can leaders prepare for such a VUCA future? Crossing the chasm from VUCA to VUCA Prime requires a different mindset.

Neuroscience research suggests that one of the most significant impediments to change is the assumption that what worked in the past will also work in the future. In *Mindset*,[45]Carol Dweck differentiates between a fixed mindset (one that gets stuck in the present) and a more forward thinking "growth" mindset.

A fixed mindset fears failure. It avoids challenges. It ignores feedback. It leads to a desire to look smart and protect one's image. It longs for the day when you can look back and rest on your laurels. A growth mindset, on the other hand, embraces change and challenge. It doesn't avoid challenge, but chases it. It sees failure as a stepping stone for future success and feels life is a journey that is always just 1% complete.

A growth mindset is critical to succeed and thrive in a VUCA world. At the organizational level, VUCA Prime-savvy leaders embrace volatility, uncertainty, complexity, and ambiguity with courage, confidence, and empowerment. At a personal level, VUCA Prime-savvy individuals demonstrate the ability to be fully present, mindful, and attentive to the stream of information that flows to them and respond accordingly.

The Prepared Mind of a Leader breaks down the growth mindset further. Its premise is even more relevant today than when I first read it in 2006 while completing my Master's Degree. The authors delineate eight fundamental skills for a "Prepared Mind":[46]

OBSERVING

The environment in which we live and operate is constantly changing. It's natural for us to look for confirming information about our view of the world, but it's often more important to look for disconfirming information. What are you observing lately?

Reasoning

People will want to know why you are proposing a course of action and will not follow your lead until they understand your explanation. What are your answers to the "why" question?

Imagining

The future is unknowable, but it can be visualized. Established industries, companies, policies, practices, etc. are always challenged by new (imagined) ideas. What's running through your mind these days?

Challenging

Any organization's business is built on assumptions. When was the last time you challenged your assumptions and tested their validity?

Deciding

Face it: you get paid to make or influence decisions because action is essential to progress. Are you progressing or paralyzed?

Learning

Past knowledge got you to where you are today. It may or may not be effective in continuing to move you forward. What don't you know that you should?

ENABLING

You may be smart, but progress requires a concerted effort for any organization. Do the people around you have the knowledge and the means and, most importantly, the opportunity to progress?

REFLECTING

All decisions have trade-offs. We need to look at past decisions and understand the trade-offs we made and the consequences of those trade-offs. We also need to reflect-forward (envision) and consider the trade-offs we are about to make. The problem is that we are time-starved and never seem to have the time to "just think." Have you spent any time quietly thinking lately?

During exponential change, a leader's most important asset is his (or her) ability to anticipate and adapt quickly. He is expected to know what to keep and what to change. He constantly must walk a thin line between thinking and doing, responding and reacting, planning and experimenting. The authors explained it this way:

Prepared minds know how to engage in thoughtful, real-time observation, analysis, and decision making in the midst of time sensitive, resource constrained, high risk situations and know how to keep themselves and those around them focused on their core purpose and ultimate goals.[47]

While that is certainly a mouthful, it pretty much sums up the current and future state of leadership. The prepared mind, however, is not for leaders only. After years on a job, it is natural for tasks to become routine. You internalize what has to be done. You begin to perform much of your job on auto-pilot. You no longer need to think how to do the job. You become fast and efficient. You become the go-to-person and expert … and you may even begin to believe all the hyperbole draped upon you.

You start to ignore the changes around you and ignore the small symptoms and consequences of change. You become so busy maintaining the status quo and making little tweaks when only necessary that you ignore the elephant standing in the room. You've become very efficient at what you do today but stop preparing for the future. You start thinking, "I'll believe it when I see it, because I believe I see it."

Alternatively, the prepared mind actively observes what's going on and seeks to understand it. He resists the urge to just hunker down and hopes change passes over. He lives with the need to:

1. Sense the environment and changes.

2. Make sense of the input.

3. Decide on an appropriate correction action.

4. Act on that decision.

Many leaders perform the first three behaviors remarkably well. They observe a problem and then make sense of it, but fail to pull the trigger in time. In years gone by, when change occurred at a comfortable pace, the consequences of delay were minimal. There was often enough time to catch your breath before embarking on another round of disruptive activity. Today, volatility breeds uncertainty and complexity which requires continuous observation, sensing, decision-making, and action.

Many of the winners in the Age of Exponential Change haven't revealed themselves yet. In fact, many of the winners aren't even in the marketplace yet. It is, however, likely that many of today's winners who don't respond and react quickly will be among the big losers in the decade ahead. Which side will you be on?

VUCA is here. It's real. It represents opportunity or chaos, abundance or emptiness. The clock is ticking. The choices are clear and decisions are yours to make. Think with a growth mindset and a prepared mind.

Key Points

» Preparing to lead in VUCA world requires a different mindset.

» A fixed mindset fears failure. A growth mindset embraces challenge and change.

» The prepared mind observes, makes sense, decides, and acts.

Questions:

» What have I observed lately that seems a bit odd?

» How could these events, problems, or issues impact my future?

» What am I seeing that I'm denying because it doesn't fit in my view of the world?

» Can I afford to ignore this?

» What don't I know but should?

» Am I listening to the people closest to the problem or the opportunity?

» What can I do better?

JOBS AND THE REWORK OF WORK

CREATING MORE JOBS is at the top of a lot of people's minds. Politicians promise new jobs. Employers offer them. Workers want them. And yet everyone seems to be spinning their wheels. Why?

First, we need to stop kidding ourselves. Most of us treat exponential change like a family pet, when it is a humongous elephant in the room. It's not just that the scope and acceleration of this change verges on fantasy—it's getting eerie and weird too. These changes are sending shockwaves up to the boardroom and down to the production floor.

It's time to stop tiptoeing around the elephant, and confront what exponential change means for business, for work and for jobs. San Francisco employment attorney Garry Mathiason, who recently formed the first-of-its-kind *Robotics, Artificial Intelligence and Automation Practice Group* at Littler Mendelson, the nation's largest employment law firm, suggests that it seems: "We are walking from the pages of science fiction into the workplace." He may not be exaggerating.

For most of us, exponential change of this magnitude happens once-in-a-lifetime. We're all novices when it comes to navigating the new labor markets and workplaces. We would have to go back to the invention of the wheel, printing press, steam engine, and electricity to find comparable disruption in how work gets done. It is highly improbable that anyone reading this was around to experience the "gut-wrenching transformation" of jobs when humans transitioned from farms to factories in the mid-19th century.[48]

More recently, Baby Boomers and older generations may equate today's disruption with the significant turmoil in labor markets in the 1970s and 1980s. Computers, automation, and a wave of outsourcing displaced millions of people from their jobs. Concurrent with this technological and functional job shift, there was a transformation of women at work. The female participation rate (ages 25—54) soared from an average of 36% in 1950 to nearly 64% in 1980 (and over 80% by 2015). During the same time period, the share of prime-age men (ages 25—54) who were neither working nor looking for work doubled.[49] While millions of labor-intensive manufacturing jobs were eliminated or shipped overseas, even more new technology and service jobs were created. Disruptions in the labor market soon became normalized and that is the biggest threat to workers today. The expectation is that this next work revolution will look and feel just like the last one. Unfortunately, with exponential change, the speed and scope of change doesn't start at zero, but launches from where the last shift ended. In other words, the magnitude of change ahead related to how work will get done and the types of jobs it creates will make today's world pale in comparison to the new normal we will know tomorrow.

Futurist Edward Gordon identifies four such comparable times in human history. They produced five labor market eras: pre-historic, agricultural, industrial, computer, and the emerging cyber-mental age. Each era witnessed significant shifts in society, family, employment, education, and quality of life. What is most notable however is that while the agrarian age lasted nearly 70 centuries (5,000 B.C.—1850 A.D.), the industrial era ran its course in 150 years (1850—1970). Today we are witnessing the end of the computer era (1970—2010) after just 40 years, and we welcome the beginning what Gordon calls the Cyber-Mental Age, a world of work where the lines between machines and humans blur. As significant and breathtaking as the concept cyber-mental is, I believe the disruption is much bigger than that and prefer to call it an era of Exponential Change.

Before we can fully understand the scope of disruption and how it will impact jobs and labor, it is important to ask ourselves this crucial and fundamental question: ***"Why do we work?"***

The idea of work for pay—a job—is a relatively recent phenomenon. Prior to the 19th century, the concept of a job as we've come to know it was not something you chose to do. That all changed in the 1800s with the Industrial Revolution. Before that, people fended for themselves mostly as artisans and craftsmen or performed work as slaves for masters. Improvement in the quality of life was up to the discretion of others. While working harder might have garnered recognition, it did not change your societal status or buy your independence.

This modern version of a job adopted by industry in the early to mid-20th century evolved from the Alfred P. Sloan scientific management philosophy of organizational design. Michael Chui, Senior Fellow with McKinsey, succinctly describes the Sloan Age as:

The best way to harness human talent [was] through full-time, exclusive employment relationships where people [were] paid for the amount of time they spent at a common location. They [were] organized in stable hierarchies where they [were] evaluated primarily through the judgment of their superiors, and what and how they [did] their jobs [was] prescribed.

This version of work is intricately linked to a mindset of scarcity. Ask an individual why he works and you'll likely hear "to pay bills" or maybe "save for retirement" or "send our kids to school." In other words, we work and seek jobs to survive because in a world of scarcity we need food, clothing and shelter to continue living. We could try to produce all those primary needs ourselves, as people did for millennia before us, but it's far easier to get a job to earn enough money to buy those things from others.

We've become so good at working that many of us have income left over for entertainment and other non-essential purchases, especially when compared to billions of people in undeveloped and under-developed countries. This free market system produces abundant and inexpensive consumer goods and services. It makes more sense for each of us to sell our skills rather than try to produce and make everything for ourselves. This is the foundation and beauty of capitalism. It is this current concept of work and jobs as we know them, linchpins of modern life that is under attack.

Until recently, this model has worked beautifully. But the schema of work and organization are being shattered by disruptive technologies, networks, and globalization. What happens when more work can be done with fewer people? What happens when we don't need people to fill all the jobs? What happens to all the people who are programmed to live with a mindset of scarcity and are dependent on jobs for survival?

Those are troubling questions to ask and even more problematic to answer without a robust public discussion. Whether we choose to embrace or ignore exponential change, the implications of it are not hypothetical anymore. Its impact is very real.

Exponential change that disrupts work is not a passing fad either. Our world will never rebound to its prior state. As the concept of work gets re-worked, jobs are changed too. Old jobs disappear. New jobs emerge that require new, more advanced skills. A new normal is then established which redefines how work gets done and who does it.

Despite some early rough patches, the evolution from industrial-age jobs to service and knowledge was fundamentally incremental and steady. Then the Great Recession of 2008 drove the final nail into the old-school job coffin. Since then, any job that could be completed by performing a series of repetitive tasks finds itself on the verge of extinction. Telemarketers, tax preparers, bookkeeping clerks, bank tellers, and secretaries will likely meet the same fate as the lector, iceman and sewing-machine operator.[50] The ability to use your head as well as your hands, not one or the other, is a requirement for almost any job today—at least those paying a good living wage.

Marc Pensky coined an eloquent phrase "digital immigrant" to describe the current state of the average worker, "People will always be behind now, and that will be a stress they have to cope with."[51] That stress is unequivocally pervasive among Baby Boomers and Generation X, who have experienced this exponential acceleration of changing technology only as adults. Thomas Friedman captures how different life used to be when he writes about what it was like to grow up in the mid to late 20th century in his newest book, *Thank You for Being Late*:

You could lead a decent lifestyle as an average worker, with an average high school or four-year college education, belonging to an average union or none at all. And just by working an average of 5 days a week at an average of 8 hours a day, you could buy an average house, have an average of 2.0 kids, visit Disney World occasionally, and save for an average retirement.[52]

He followed this with:

Today's American Dream is now more of a journey than a final destination—and one that increasingly feels like walking up a down escalator.[53]

Reliance on technology and automation evokes a sense of dependability and anxiety in the 40+ age group. For Millennials and Generation Z, exposure to technology began at birth, and the relationship is intimately personal. With this changing of the guard in the workforce, a new norm is developing especially in the career-work-job landscape. This shift empowers and instills freedom in Millennials and Generation Z.

It's not just that jobs are changing, but job classifications are changing too. A popular estimate suggests that 65% of children entering primary school today will ultimately end up working in completely new job types that don't yet exist.[54] That's preposterous to a Boomer or Gen X, but completely normal to our younger generations. The need for permanent full-time workers is disappearing too. That's been the trend since the late 1990s in the U.S. and many developed economies and will continue as legacy companies automate, downsize, or disappear.

Workers of all ages are adapting to this new world of work too. Unlike the past, when working part-time was a stepping stone to full-time employment or a means to propping up personal finances, part-time work in the future will be by design. Many workers often juggle multiple jobs with several employers at the same time by choice.

With the Millennials and Generation Z soon to be 75% of the workforce, freelancing and contingent work will become the norm. It simply fits their more flexible and mobile lifestyle and offers significant advantages to employers too. Freelancing may be the preferred career path for as much as 50% of the workforce by 2020. And by 2025, employers and employees will choose this type of employer-employee engagement over the more traditional full-time and part-time classification. The contingent, freelancing, "just-in-time" worker will replace the full time and part-time employee as the most common type on the payroll.

It doesn't end there. Employees often don't "go to work" either. Telecommuting and remote work is growing exponentially, too. Workers in almost every walk of life simultaneously interact with different teams on different projects with various customers in multiple locations. Workplace issues like accommodation for the physically impaired or disabled are becoming a non-factor because location just doesn't matter anymore. Skilled workers, including attorneys, accountants, and engineers, work remotely just as ubiquitously as programmers and developers work today. Even surgeons are starting to perform surgeries with advanced robotics on patients who are located thousands of miles away.

R.I.P. TO THE WAY IT WAS

It goes without saying that an epic shift is underway. From social media to the Internet of Things, digital fabrication to robotics, virtual reality to synthetic biology, new technologies are rewriting the playbook for securing jobs, managing people, and leading organizations.

> ### TIP OF THE ICEBERG!
>
> SUPERMARKETS USED TO EMPLOY 30 HUMANS TO CHECKOUT CUSTOMERS. NOW ONE HUMAN OVERSEES 30 CASHIER ROBOTS. MORE CUSTOMERS GET SERVED IN LESS TIME WITH FEWER ERRORS.
>
> ROBOTS CAN WELD AND PAINT CARS NOW. THERE IS NO REASON THEY WON'T BE COOKING FOOD IN RESTAURANTS, PICKING FRUITS, SWEEPING FLOORS AND VIRTUALLY ANYTHING ELSE IMAGINABLE.
>
> HOSPITALS ARE USING ROBOTS TO DISPENSE MEDICINE. ROBOTS ARE REPLACING PARALEGALS AND A ROBOT WAS JUST INSTALLED THAT HANDLES BANKRUPTCY LAW.
>
> SALES ROBOTS ARE COMING TO LOWE'S HOME CENTER STORES. ROBOTS ARE INTERVIEWING JOB CANDIDATES, AND COVERING THE NEWS AND SPORTS.
>
> GOLDMAN SACH'S NEW YORK HEADQUARTERS REPLACED 600 STOCK TRADERS WITH 200 COMPUTER ENGINEERS.

For some of you, it may feel as if you are staring into the light of an accelerating oncoming locomotive. Today is the future that was forecast for decades but you hoped never came. Unfortunately, time has run out. For others, this shift is the light at the end of the tunnel following years of anticipation. Hope and opportunity wait. Reality is ready to run right over those clinging to the status quo and to reward those who see possibilities.

What does this mean for managers of business and employees seeking jobs?

1. **It means there is no going back.** We live in a world with changing labor markets, a changing workforce, and even the changing nature of work—changes that are unfolding right before our wondering eyes. The default presumption that employers offer jobs that are long-term, full-time, and on-site with vertical career paths is history. Employment relationships will be increasingly short-term, transactional, and unpredictable.

2. **Anything can become obsolete at any time.** The pace of technological advances and disruption is unprecedented — and not just in the computing world. Every aspect of our lives and our businesses can be impacted without notice. Think communication, transportation, entertainment, medicine, education. Companies continually restructure, re-engineer, downsize, merge, or acquire. Everything and everyone is vulnerable. Who ever imagined that venerable institutions, including states and countries, could run out of money and declare bankruptcy?

3. **Job security is history.** Continuous employment by one employer is dead. Organizations eliminate and remodel jobs in response to shifts in the markets. The loss of jobs today isn't an act of disloyalty but a response to change. Ensuring you have the right people in the right place at the right time means adopting more efficient and dependable ways to access talent.

4. **The free agent mindset rules.** Without credible long-term promises and job security from employers, employees are learning to live one day at a time. Free agency is no longer a stigma; it's a career strategy. Baby Boomers seek free

agency because they expect to be active and work long after traditional retirement. Millennials and Generation Z have never known anything but free agency.

5. **Managing people will only get harder.** It's always been hard to manage people. There have always been people of all types and generations working side by side in the workplace. But today there are as many as six generations sharing the workplace. Generational gaps merely skim the surface of how different the workforce is and will be. Diversity, gender equality, income inequality, sexual preference, and skill gaps exponentially increase the number of issues confronting managers each day, not to mention run-of-the mill interpersonal differences. It's like the potential for disruption and distraction has been injected with steroids. It's no wonder that people management has become a thriving and growing industry!

6. **Churn and squeeze.** With fewer long-term traditional employees, a revolving door will become the norm. Every person from the senior executive to the warehouse worker will be required to produce more work faster with fewer resources. Organizations will have to staff-up (and down) quickly while, at the same time, acquiring a higher quality worker. To be competitive, real-time data from people analytics will be as essential to management as the air we breathe.

That's just a few ways the business playbook is being rewritten these days. Maybe Isaac Asimov had it right when he said:

It is change, continuing change, inevitable change that is the dominant factor in society today. No sensible decision can be made any longer without taking into account not only the world as it is, but the world as it will be ... This, in turn, means that our statesmen, our businessmen, our everyman must take on a science fictional way of thinking.

Use Your Imagination

The probability that any job will go unscathed by advances in automation is small to non-existent. The overarching question everyone should be asking is "when and how much will my job and the jobs of my employees, co-workers, and family be changed in the next few years?" Exact dates and times are still up for grabs but based on most projections, disruption is much closer than we think.

1. To prepare start by asking these questions:
   » What jobs will be affected first?
   » When will I feel the first effects?
   » How will I know it's time to rethink my career?

2. Familiarize yourself with the most common technologies that are disrupting careers:
   » Artificial intelligence (AI)
   » Robots
   » Sensors
   » 3D Printing

3. Then ask:
   » Which technology is most likely to disrupt my job?
   » Will the technology make my job obsolete or just change the way work gets done?
   » What new skills will I need to learn to co-work with a machine?

EXAMPLE: HOW HVAC TECHNICIANS CAN STEP INTO THE FUTURE

For approximately the next five years, the U.S. will need one additional heating/ventilation/air-conditioning (HVAC) technician for every five technicians already working.[55] This is nearly double the growth rate of all jobs through 2022. What happens after that?

The good news is that on midnight, January 1, 2023, no one is flipping a switch that turns HVAC technicians into a bunch of pumpkins. The bad news is that one well-known study suggests a 65% probability that HVAC technician jobs will be significantly automated by 2030. What might the new version of HVAC technician look like?

The HVAC technician of the future will likely be a network or computer engineer who just happens to be working in the HVAC industry. Smart technologies and the Internet of Things (IoT) will continue to evolve as sensors are integrated into every room in our homes and office buildings. Integrating all this technology into a reliable and consumer friendly experience will require more than mechanical skills. Like the homeowner who can pull up an app to adjust his residential thermostat and check on his home, technicians too will monitor their clients' sensors remotely, maintaining the system and troubleshooting problems without any owner engagement. If a problem does require an on-site visit, the technician will signal one of the company's autonomous vehicles in the area and dispatch it to you.

It won't be long until the sensor dispatches the vehicle by itself. Once onsite, a robot exits the vehicle to inspect the HVAC unit. It diagnoses the problem and triggers the 3D printer in the truck to start fabricating a replacement part. The robot retrieves the part and places it in the unit. The technician, still monitoring the system from the office, guides the robot in making all the proper connections. When complete, the technician runs another set of diagnostics and releases the robot and his vehicle for another call. If by chance, the part could not be fabricated by a 3D printer, the technician could release a drone to transport the part to the site.

Will technology obviate the HVAC technician by 2023? It's not only highly unlikely, but improbable. But if I was a HVAC tech today and hoping to still have an HVAC job in 2030, I'd be very worried. Moving forward, there will be no such thing as resting on your laurels. Five or ten years of experience working with mechanical motors and parts will mean nothing when HVAC technologies like 3D-printed evaporative-cooling bricks cool and warm rooms with nothing but water and air.[56]

HVAC technicians are not alone in their fight to stay relevant. How will AI, robots, sensors, and 3D printers threaten or enhance your job by 2020? Will you even recognize your job by 2030?

KEY POINTS

» History has produced 4 labor market eras. We are transitioning to the 5th.

» The concept of modern day work is under attack.

» It's not just job titles that are coming and going but job classifications too.

» Employees don't "go to work" anymore.

» For employees, free agency will rule. For managers, your job will only get harder.

QUESTIONS FOR EMPLOYERS

» How prepared are your managers to lead a contingent and/or remote team?

» How prepared are your managers to lead a blended workforce of full-time, contingent, and robotic workers?

» How will managing a blended workforce of full-time, contingent, and robotic workers impact human resources policies?

QUESTIONS FOR WORKERS

» How prepared are you to manage a career as a contingent worker?

» How prepared are you to work remotely on projects as well as collaborate locally with multiple teams on an as-needed basis?

» How will you market yourself to secure a continuous flow of job opportunities?

Average is Officially Over

I'M ASKED THIS QUESTION over and over by worried parents, grandparents, teachers, and sometimes on behalf of the proverbial "friend": "What are the essential skills that my [fill the blank with kid, grandkid, students, self, etc.] will need to have to make it in tomorrow's workplace?"

The question is not new. What has changed recently is the frequency of conversations like this. The tone is starting to sound a bit more desperate, too. And the age of the adult seeking such advice is getting older.

It's no wonder. As you read in a previous chapter, the world of work and jobs is in a state of flux. Uncertainty is abundant. At the epicenter of this change is technology. For hundreds of years, human workers were the "computers," conducting research and making calculations. Even when electronic computers arrived in the 1940s, they were assistants to the workers. People still did everything but crunch the numbers. But the arrival of artificial intelligence and machine learning now threatens the role of humans as workers. Moshe Vardi recently told the American Association for the Advancement of Science that "we are approaching the time when machines will be able to outperform humans at almost any task."[57]

What makes the future even more ambiguous is that jobs are being lost faster than new jobs are being created. I'm not talking about the rise and fall of available jobs we see during conventional economic booms and busts. I'm talking about millions of jobs disappearing literally, going extinct.

All this change puts average workers with average skills smack in the crosshairs of disruption. "It's really, really, going to be difficult to be a worker in this world," says Thomas Friedman. "Average is officially over ... This is creating huge anxiety out there in every one of your labor forces."[58]

If true (and no one should have any reason to believe otherwise), average skills will qualify workers for only a small subset of jobs going forward and the growth of these jobs is shrinking fast. Up until the 1960s, the worker with average skills was on equal footing with more skilled workers and many professionals to reach a middle income or higher lifestyle. Most jobs required only a high school education. Today, average skills and a high school diploma lead down a crowded pathway of low-skill, low-pay jobs. Those opportunities are shrinking too.

Edward Gordon, author of *Winning the Global Talent Showdown*, projects that low-paying, low-skill jobs will shrink to just 26% of the total jobs in the U.S. What's more troubling is that just 44 million people will be needed for those jobs, but 150 million or more candidates will be seeking those jobs.[59] A downward trend in new job creation in new technology industries is particularly evident starting in the Computer Revolution of the 1980s. For example, a study by Jeffery Lin suggests that while about 8.2% of the U.S. workforce shifted into new jobs during the 1980s which were associated with new technologies; during the 1990s this figure declined to 4.4%. Estimates by Thor Berger and Carl Benedikt Frey further suggest that less than 0.5% of the U.S. workforce shifted into technology industries that emerged throughout the 2000s, including new industries such as online auctions, video and audio streaming, and web design.[60]

Even top-tier professions like law, medicine, engineering, and accounting are being replaced by algorithms, artificial intelligence, robots, and software.

This is a far cry from the not-so-distant past when a high school diploma reserved a spot with the middle class. After that, all that was needed was hard work and conscientiousness. You could hold a job for a lifetime by just showing up. Improving an employee's intellectual or problem-solving capacity was something most employers did not want and employees did not need.

Then technology came along and made each human more productive. It was the equivalent of attaching a super-charged battery to the backs of each employee. With more productivity, more products could be made cheaper which increased consumer demand. With increased demand, even technology-enabled humans could not keep up. More humans were hired.

Aspirations for advancement could even be a career derailer for the average worker in many companies and industries. The more self-motivation a worker had, the more likely he or she would want to move up or out if given an opportunity, leaving a vacancy to be filled. Since turnover, for whatever reason, was viewed as a bad thing, it was in the company's best interest to suppress personal growth. Some employers baited workers with a nominal wage increase and withheld training due to a fear that a better-trained and experienced employee might jump ship to a competitor.

Things have changed and today, employers need workers who are agile, adept, and have a passionate desire to learn and grow. More thinking capacity isn't just desired, it is essential. It is the one resource that most organizations can't get enough of.

Job seekers need to think in terms of what it will take to find a job, hold a job, and advance in a job even when that job is a constantly moving object. With accelerating change, the skills one needs today may be irrelevant tomorrow. Richard K Miller, President of Olin College of Engineering, describes today's job environment as "marching into a forest that no one has explored in search of things you have never seen ... [searching for] jobs you can't imagine..."[61]

That shift from brawn power to brain power also requires a massive shift in mindset. The Institute for the Future (IFTF) released research that suggests that a qualitative shift, perhaps an order of magnitude greater than the outsourcing revolution, could now be taking shape in the workforce.[62] Nurturing a growth mindset[63]—the belief that talent and abilities can be expanded with dedication and hard work compared to the you-are-either-smart-or-dumb fixed mindset—is a vital ingredient for future success. A growth mindset expands capacity, adds value, and is an indispensable foundation to innovate and grow an organization. The growth mindset is foreign territory for millions of people and many organizations.

Whether you're an executive in a Fortune 100 company, the owner of a small business, or a worker seeking a new job, the focus must shift to skills, not jobs. Economist James Bessen, a researcher and lecturer at Boston University School of Law, concludes that "Jobs are not going away but the needed skills for good jobs are going up. And with the new technology platform we're now on, it's all happening faster."[64]

Creating a short list of skills that any one worker needs to thrive and prosper in the era of exponential change is a daunting task. It would be pointless to even promote such a list as definitive and conclusive. But through personal experience and meta-research, it is safe to say that the following six skills provide a blueprint for almost every worker and any job—at least for the next decade or two.

Admittedly, few jobs will require a high level of proficiency in all six skills. But everyone will need to be at least comfortable with each one. As artificial intelligence, machine learning, and robotics improve, it's safe to say that the only thing standing in a worker's way of being replaced with machine or software will be how well he or she has honed these skills.

1. CURIOSITY

Curiosity is as important as intelligence.[65] The Oxford Dictionary defines curiosity as "a strong desire to know or learn something." I'm going to take it one step further and suggest that it may be more important than intelligence because the by-product of curiosity is knowledge, and knowledge improves intelligence. In a world characterized by persistent change, uncertainty, complexity, and ambiguity, curiosity may be the one coping skill everyone needs to survive and thrive in this type of environment.

2. CREATIVITY

Creativity is a word that gets bounced around in today's workplace like a Super Ball. Some praise it as the cure for our future and others claim it to be a massive distraction and threat. I'm in the former school.

My definition of creativity is the ability to generate new ideas and turn them into solutions, the ability to see the world in a new way, the ability to connect the dots in ways that others have missed. I'll be the first to admit this definition isn't perfect. To tie creativity to solutions may be too restrictive. To claim it connects the dots may limit how far it can extend. However, in the context of job skills, my definition of creativity describes an absolutely critical skill in the business world.

3. CONSCIENTIOUSNESS

A staggering amount of research links conscientiousness with success, regardless of the employee's role or the employer's industry.[66] An employer regards conscientious Average Joe (or Sue) as a dependable, responsible, organized, and proactive employee. He arrives on time, stays late, does his work, meets deadlines, exercises good self-control, and manages himself well.

But conscientiousness may not be a skill at all. It may be a trait that's the product of genetics and environment. How do you increase or improve conscientiousness? Can you train people in it? The truth is, conscientiousness is probably a combination of genetic hard wiring, environmental influences, skill training, and motivation. And this is good news given how needed and how critical it is to the 21st century workplace.

4. CRITICAL THINKING

In the not too distant past, brawn power was more important than brain power in the workplace, and Average Joe was told to check his critical thinking at the door. He was expected to follow instructions, not ask too many questions, remember and understand what he was taught, and repeat it over and over again.

Then change showed up and knocked on the manager's door. Now Joe's critical thinking is a highly desirable, and even essential, skill. His workplace needs his ability to analyze, evaluate, and create, especially because his organization is leaner now. He has more responsibilities to carry out with fewer resources, and management's expectations are higher. He's expected to think analytically and apply the results of that thinking, all without benefit of instruction or supervision.

5. Collaboration

No, collaboration is not just a new buzz word for teamwork. It's much more sophisticated than that. Organizations are shifting from a hierarchical top-down structure to a network of teams. And thanks to technology, the internet, globalization, and mobility, Joe may be working with team members he's never met. Team members will be selected by their ability to contribute and the value they add, not because of their job title, department, tenure, or even geography. A 30-year veteran may be assigned the lead on one team while he reports to a just-hired Millennial on another.

Chances are, those team members will come and go, along with expertise brought in from the outside in order to complete a project. Plus, the day is not far off when one of those team members may not even be human! The ability to collaborate with other people tests the resolve of many. It won't be long until robots like IBM Watson, Baxter[67] or ROSS[68] become your partner. In this ever-changing, complex environment, Joe's ability to keep the wheels of his employer's business moving because he's a skilled collaborator will be highly sought after.

6. AGILITY

Can anyone argue that the ability to keep pace, to shift gears often and quickly, and to keep current with the flow of information is not a skill in hot demand? Unfortunately agility is a crucial skill that fewer and fewer people have. In fact, there probably isn't a human on this planet who isn't struggling somewhat with the exponential rate of change they are experiencing.

But speed alone doesn't do justice to the high level of skill Joe really needs. Agility is the ability to move nimbly and to think and draw conclusions, accurate ones, quickly. This combination requires Joe possess not just a high personal energy level, but also fast cognitive abilities so he can perform well in many jobs and functions if that's what his company culture demands. The more aggressive, dynamic, and growth-driven an organization, the more agility matters.

So, there you have it—curiosity, creativity, conscientiousness, critical thinking, collaboration, and agility. These are the six essential skills Joe, along with millions of workers, will need in order to be a success in the 21st century workplace. These are the skills that will make the difference in growth versus stagnation, jobs versus unemployment, and meaningful versus trivial work in the environment of exponential change that is facing the business world.

KEY POINTS

» Average workers with average skills are in the crosshairs of disruption.

» Professional jobs are as vulnerable as blue collar ones.

» Focus on skills, not jobs.

» Teams will be formed based on individual ability and value contributors add, not job title and tenure.

QUESTIONS

» What happens when machines can outperform most humans?

» What are the skills that organizations need to grow and succeed in the future?

» How will you choose between hiring a human or employing a machine?

» How will you select members for teams?

EDUCATION-TO-EMPLOYMENT PATHWAY IS BROKEN

THE TRADITIONAL EDUCATION-TO-EMPLOYMENT pathway is experiencing an all-out assault on its credibility. Only half of employers believe college graduates are ready to work compared to nearly 9 out of 10 graduates who feel they can jump right in.[69] Another survey by McKinsey and Co. affirmed the fundamental disconnect between employer demands and our system of higher education: Only 42% of executives believe that students entering the workforce are prepared for the available jobs. Even worse, only 45% of these young people think that they are prepared.

More troubling is that nearly half of all students who start a bachelor's degree program fail to complete it, leaving them deep in debt with nothing to show for it. Many graduates aren't faring much better, when they can't get jobs, or do find them but are under-employed. The college degree, which historically was the currency we exchanged for opportunity, has lost its luster despite coming with a very steep price tag.

How did this disconnect happen? As our world continues to evolve at lightning speed, it's easy to blame disruptive technology for changing what we once loved. Depending upon your viewpoint, responsibility can be placed on the shoulders of helicopter parents who raised a generation of trophy kids, at educators out of touch with the needs of business, at bureaucrats consumed with preserving the status quo, and at politicians more concerned with re-election than re-engineering. Workers too deserve their fair share of blame—from the entitlement attitude of the baby boomer to the immediate-gratification-driven millennial.

Exponential change also contributes to the education-to-employment disconnect. Think about this: The time to complete a degree is four years; the rate of change of technology and economic cycles is six months to two years; and the majority of students graduate with the "wrong" degrees for the job market. The "right" degrees aren't known or may not even exist when students start college. The phenomenal rate that technology grows is already highlighting a skills shortage where students often know more about the emerging technology than their teachers who were not raised on five screens.[70]

This begs the question: Why are businesses still using the college degree as a primary criterion for hiring when the evidence for their predictability is so low?

The good news is that despite all the controversy, nearly everyone agrees that we need a shorter, less expensive learning pathway to employment. Education in general is moving away from its conventional once-and-done infusion of knowledge to a commitment of continuous lifelong learning. Individuals and organizations want to be able to "purchase" what they need, when they need it. Community colleges and some universities have responded on a case-by-case basis, but it is unlikely they can turn their ships around fast enough to meet the crippling job skills crisis. The search is on for a solution and from all indications it will likely come from outside the traditional education system.

This shift gives rise to new companies and new job preparedness models offering a blend of formal, informal, and corporate learning that align with strategic goals of businesses.[71]

A strong case can be made to replace the current system of diplomas, degrees, and certifications with competency-based selection, learning, and development. But while answers like this may seem easy, the challenges are quite complex. Agreement is high on the benefits and rationale for change; but solving the education-to-employment disconnect is equally as complex as solving the problems as associated with the cost and access to healthcare. Focusing on these 3 questions is a great place to start.

"Which credentials matter?" In today's job market, the shelf-life of in-demand skill is about 5 years. A popular estimate is that 65% of all new jobs in the next 5 years don't exist yet. That means that schools and training providers have to adapt quickly to market fluctuations and individuals must reskill and upskill continuously. That's a far cry from just a few years ago when education ended with graduation and decades of work followed.

Educational credentials are still a viable currency to qualify employees and secure work, but employers are going to have to get a lot better at identifying exactly what skills, abilities, and training lead to the best outcomes. What data is being collected that is useful and predictive? For now, degrees, years of experience, and most performance ratings are just crude proxies for hiring and skill development. To remain competitive, employers will need to send the right and timely signals to colleges and non-traditional training programs who can respond with relevant and responsive job preparation.

The second question is *"What credentials will companies recognize?"* Despite the lack of trust in the education system, that hasn't stopped many organizations from using the college degree as a prerequisite for employment. Currently, more than 6 out of every 10 posted jobs require postsecondary education,[72] but only 1/3 of the people have a bachelor's degree or higher.[73] Part of the problem is that employers don't really know what skills they're looking for. The associate and bachelor degree is used as a proxy to screen out a glut of unqualified applicants coming from online job postings.[74]

While somewhat effective at saving managers from interviewing applicants with a poor fit, "up-credentialing" is not an effective approach for attracting or identifying more skilled workers. It is just as likely to increase the risk of shutting out the right ones.

Research from Innovate+Educate showed that only 1% of disconnected young adults aged 16-24 could qualify for a job based on a degree requirement, but nearly one-third of them have the skills and abilities to do the job.[75] This credential inflation is affecting a wide range of jobs, from executive assistants to production, distribution and construction supervisors. Seeking candidates with advanced degrees for work that requires only a high school diploma, certification or some college is like purchasing a bulldozer when all you need is a shovel. In a tight labor market, that's a no-no.

The 3rd question is *"How will candidates and employees be credentialed?"* I mentioned earlier that a solution might come from outside the bureaucracy of traditional education—schools and colleges. Progressive and innovative companies aren't waiting around. Digital badges may soon carry as much credibility as an academic degree. Combined with competency-specific skill assessments, portfolios of work, apprenticeships, and work experience, employers will be able to target more desirable candidates in a larger, more diverse talent pool while today's worker will have more choices of credentials to prove their fitness for a job. Offsite classrooms are being replaced by boot camps, learning accelerators, and social learning. Just-in-time learning helps employees move into new roles faster and learn new skills on their own.

It is not just speed and relevance of education that matters; it is the cost of education and work preparedness too. The cost of higher education is a huge impediment to accessing more skilled workers. In true entrepreneurial fashion, competitive pressure is coming from MOOCs (Massive Open Online Courses) that include free classes from institutions like Stanford, MIT, Harvard, UC Berkeley, Duke, and Carnegie Mellon. They provide a world-class education for close to nothing. Access to MOOCs and other variations of inexpensive online learning (including YouTube and iTunes) is forcing traditional degree programs to be unbundled. Skill specific content is made available on a large scale at lower cost.

It won't be long until alternatives to 120 credits and 4 years of time are accepted as education-based proof of competency. Going forward, a company's best candidates may come from workers who never attended college or technical schools but learned skills through non-traditional pathways and demonstrates proficiency with a portfolio of badges.

This too, is also worth considering. Maybe—just maybe—the job skill shortage isn't as bad as many employers claim it to be.

What if skilled labor was sitting under your nose, but arbitrary credential and screening filters hid qualified candidates from view? Taking advantage of non-traditional pathways to employment does not lower the bar for candidates but raises the standard by which organizations hire. Competency- and evidence-based hiring forces HR and hiring managers to get their acts together. It requires them to rely more on the evidence that drives employee success and less on degrees, assumptions, and gut instinct. Old habits are tough to break but the effort is well worth it. Setting practical credentialing standards and opening up non-traditional pathways to employment expands job search to populations that were once ignored and where more talent resides.

There is a downside to digital badges, of course. Currently there is little standardization of non-traditional credentials which creates confusion and skepticism. Badges are proliferating like ants at a picnic too. There's a huge amount of work to be done, but with maturity and wider acceptance by employers, greater trust and acceptance will come. More transparency and accurate insight on what is required to succeed will help fill positions faster with the right workers. Job seekers will be able to fast-track training and learning to meet in-demand skills.

KEY POINTS

» The traditional education-to-employment pathway needs a makeover.

» Exponential change exacerbates the education-to-employment disconnect.

» New companies and new models may replace schools and universities for job readiness.

» Digital badges and other non-traditional credentials may soon be as credible as academic degrees.

QUESTIONS FOR DISCUSSION:

» Which credentials really matter?

» What credentials should companies recognize?

» How will candidates and employees be credentialed?

» What needs to change in your business to screen, hire, and retain better workers?

It's Time to Stop Bashing Millennials

I HAVE A CONFESSION TO MAKE. I'm a recovering Millennial basher.

For nearly two decades, Millennials have garnered nearly 24/7 attention from the media. They became the trophy kids of helicopter parents and the target of disdain from managers and co-workers. As a result, consulting, speaking, and writing about Millennials (along with Baby Boomers and Generation X too) became a billion-dollar business.

For several years, I hopped on that Millennial-bashing bandwagon too, and shared tales and advice about how to manage the narcissistic, digitally-obsessed, trophy-kid generation. I even devoted a chapter or two to them in my book *Geeks, Geezers and Googlization*. But time and a blinding confrontation with the obvious forced me to see them and the world in a different way.

Since publishing *Geeks, Geezers and Googlization* in 2009, I've had thousands of interactions with these young adults, born between 1980 and 1996. Yes, it's true—the oldest Millennials are old enough to be serial entrepreneurs, business owners, managers, parents, and teachers. Without hesitation, I can say many of them have become major influences in my life and now I see the future differently.

I've been impressed and awed with the courtesy, ambition, and forward-thinking attitude of the 20-something Millennials who serve our food at restaurants while they go to school full time and juggle working at two or three jobs. Likewise, I'm a bit jealous of the savvy, hardworking, entrepreneurial recent college graduates who are wooing investors to support their new ventures, while concurrently attending class in pursuit of graduate degrees and balancing personal commitments.

For sure, some millennials fit the stereotype: self-centered, spoiled and socially immature. But so do many of my Baby Boomer peers. Just as each generation has its fair share of introverts and extroverts, slackers and winners, there's no place better to discuss entitlement than with a group of aging and retiring (or retired) Baby Boomers commiserating over young people's horrible work ethic and how great America used to be.

They seem to forget that nearly 50 years ago, Life Magazine, one of the most popular magazines of its day, introduced the "Generation Gap" to the world.[76] But they weren't talking about Millennials back then because Millennial children and grandchildren weren't even a blip on their future parents' radar yet. The "privileged, narcissistic, entitled, spoiled, lazy" young workers sullied in the press were the Baby Boomers—the original "Me Generation"[77] and same group who is currently doing a lot of griping about employees and young adults in general.

Generation X doesn't get off the hook so easy either. Equally frustrated and often resentful of the generation breathing down their necks, Gen X grabbed their share of headlines in their teen and young adult years. In December 1985, *Newsweek* hit the stands decrying "The Video Generation."[77] It read, "There they are, those preening narcissists who have to document every banal moment with their cutting-edge communications technology."

And just a few years later, *Time Magazine* ran a scathing cover story about The Next Generation, again targeting Gen X.[78] Yes, that's right. Three decades ago, Gen Xers—often the most vocal bashers of Millennials—were the brunt of everything wrong with America and now they are repulsed by the digital fixation of today's young adults. The article depicted Gen X as:

...lazy, entitled, selfish, shallow, unambitious shoe-gazers ... [who] have trouble making decisions. They would rather hike in the Himalayas than climb a corporate ladder. ...They crave entertainment, but their attention span is as short as one zap of a TV dial. ...They postpone marriage because they dread divorce. They sneer at Range Rovers and Rolexes. What they hold dear are family life, local activism, national parks, penny loafers and mountain bikes.

Doesn't that description sound familiar? With the exception of penny loafers, history seems to be repeating itself today. Maybe there is some power in the words spoken by many of our parents, "I hope your children give you the same heartache as you gave me!"

Once we cut through all of the noise, each generation begins to seem more similar than different on the big issues of life and work. Younger generations seem to catch the blame for the environment in which they grew up. Teens today didn't create the smartphone, tablet, and all of the other devices that seem to be distracting them—just as Baby Boomers didn't create the television and Gen X didn't create computers and video games. The kids didn't purchase these devices either. Their parents and grandparents did.

San Jose Public Library

Almaden Branch
6455 Camden Avenue
(408) 808-3040 or (408) 808-2000
sjpl.org
ABSELF02

Checked Out Items 2/20/2020 17:59

2185XXXXXXXXXXX1185

Item Title	Due Date
Recruiting in the age of Googlization : when the shift hits your plan / by Ira S. Wolfe. 31197016870517	3/12/2020

Total Items: 1

Amount Outstanding: $5.50

24 Hour Renewal
(408) 808-2665

DC Comics Library Card
Access FREE and exclusive benefits
with your SJPL card
(Available while supplies last)
sjpl.org/DCComics

Facebook.com/sanjoselibrary
Twitter.com/sanjoselibrary

As a recovering Millennial basher, I'm here in no uncertain terms to tell you to stop: It's time to stop bashing Millennials. It's not only a distraction, but a wasteful diversion of valuable resources away from the real culprit: exponential change. So please—no more complaining, ridiculing, mocking, and cajoling them. Millennials are not your enemy. They aren't aliens from another planet. They share the same DNA as the rest of us. They are just another generation squeezed between the older Generation X and Boomers and younger Generation Z. If fingers for their behavior and attitudes must be pointed, look in the direction of myopic bureaucrats, misguided parents, and accelerating exponential change.

Millennials didn't cause the disruption and exponential change we're experiencing any more than Baby Boomers were responsible for the baby boom of the 50s and 60s. They are just products of the time and more likely victims of the world they were born into than perpetrators. They didn't create exponential change, so stop using Millennials as the scapegoat for discomfort you're feeling due to the accelerating nature of exponential change and the explosive disruption of the status quo.

But Millennials be forewarned. There is no sulking or martyrdom allowed either. Yes, in many ways you've been screwed. You may be the first generation in recent history that isn't left better off than the previous generation. Bemoaning your plight won't lessen the pain or fix the problems. In spite of a boatload of problems, you are inheriting an enormous cache of opportunity. You are living at the footsteps of the Fourth Industrial Revolution and the rest of the world is looking to you to lead us into it.

But I digress.

To the Gen X and Baby Boomer Generation, Millennials can be your organization's most valuable allies to help lead you on a successful journey into the future. That change in attitude will, of course, require some undoing.

First, let's clear up a common problem. Most references made about Millennials, especially the derogatory ones, target the wrong age group. Since the oldest Millennial was born in 1980 and the youngest in 1996, Millennials are not today's teenagers. They aren't even the traditional first- or second-year college student. A lot of people don't realize that nearly half the Millennial population is over 30 years old, and nearly 11,000 cross that threshold each and every day. Yes, that's right—the oldest Millennials are almost 37 years old and aging.

Trying to lump 80 million people into one neat package of stereotypes is bad for business in many ways. Just as there is a big variance in Baby Boomer attitudes born in 1946 compared to those born in 1960, the same holds true for Millennials. Many Millennials excel in their jobs and contribute to the growth of organizations worldwide. They have grown to become highly productive workers, successful entrepreneurs, and valuable citizens in our communities. By bashing Millennials, managers throw out the very talent they seek in the proverbial generational bath water.

If today's adolescents, recent high school graduates, and first year college students don't belong to the Millennial Generation, who are they? Let me introduce you to Generation Z.

GENERATION Z

Generation Z, also called Gen Z and iGen, is still coming of age but smashing norms and conventions. This generation includes those young adults (and children) born between 1996 and 2010. According to the National Center for Education Statistics, there are an estimated 57 million Gen Z in the U.S. (roughly 30% smaller than Baby Boomers and Millennials and about 20% larger than Gen X). Events that have indelibly marked and shaped their young minds include school shootings, global terrorism, the Great Recession, and climate change.

Generation Z was born into a new family era in which one out of seven stay-at-home parents is a father. Compare that to the Baby Boomers, who largely grew up with one wage-earner per family and a stay-at-home mom and Gen Xers who are products of dual-career parents. Gen Z is also the first generation with parents from three generations (Boomers, Xers and Millennials). Thanks to an epidemic of Baby Boomer divorces and remarriages, delayed marriages of Generation X and a proliferation of unmarried couples and single parents, this is a generation whose familiarity with the traditional nuclear family is ensconced almost exclusively in history.

The families of Generation Z come in all colors and sizes too. This is the first generation growing up in a time when alternative lifestyles and sexual preferences are not admonished or just tolerated, but widely accepted. While Millennials grew up with friends from a diverse group of race, color and ethnicity, Gen Z have parents, family and friends whose sexual preferences are often blurred. Multi-racial children are the fastest growing youth group in the U.S.

Born at or close to the birth of the modern-day Internet, Gen Z does not know a world without technology embedded into all aspects of life. They are technologically astute and comfortable communicating at lightning speed. While most Millennials grew up with computers, keyboards, emails, and dial-up Internet access, Gen Z only knows a world of mobile devices, touchscreens, social media, apps, and high-speed connectivity. Gen Z collaborated using Google Docs at the same age that Millennials were still learning cursive.

Many of Gen Z parents have lived through multiple recessions, acquired a lifetime of debt, experienced career disruptions, and sustained periods of high unemployment. In response, Generation Z is becoming the realistic generation. If nothing else, Gen Z are learning coping skills and the power of resourcefulness. They have been taught and coached to be practical and pursue their specific strengths (unlike Millennials, who were led to believe that anything and everything was possible).

Like every generation before them, Millennials struggle with their young successors just as much as Boomers did with Gen X, and Gen X did with Millennials when they entered the workforce. Generational conflicts just go with the territory. Nevertheless, despite nearly 20 years to prepare for today's war for talent and a new generation entering the workplace, many organizations are still trying to figure out how to recruit, hire, manage, and retain Millennials—a group that now makes up the largest generation in the workforce. In just 9 more years, 75% of working-age adults will be Millennials.

It's a bit late to join the party, but as the saying goes: it's better late than never. The window of opportunity to figure out how to recruit, manage, and retain Millennials is just about shut. That means there is very little time to jump on the bandwagon and figure out what changes need to be made. Time's a wastin'.

DON'T GET ME WRONG.

I'm not discounting that the attitudes of Millennials and Gen Z can be disruptive. But what if they aren't disrupting and rebelling because they're young, but because they're right? While managers and co-workers fret about Millennials, the world is changing fast and the pace is accelerating. Just about everything Baby Boomers, Generation X, (and even the older Millennials) knew and believed about work, jobs, careers, and the workplace is significantly different than it used to be. And just as abnormal as life seems for workers in their 40s and older, this exponentially changing world is the only world they know. Instead of bashing them, embrace and engage them. It's time to use Millennials and soon Generation Z as your guides to the future, the ambassadors between our recent past and their pending future.

HERE'S THE BOTTOM LINE.

The mere fact that management and managers are just now trying to figure out Millennials is both ridiculously silly and profoundly scary. Millennials have been in the workforce for almost two decades. It's not that Millennials suddenly landed on earth and invaded the workforce. Thousands of books and articles warned of their imminent arrival. The media hasn't missed a day, or at least it seems, without a story about how Millennials are impacting the labor markets, consumer buying, and society.

Executives and managers just opted to complain about them and ignore what was going to happen when the wave of aging Baby Boomers and maturing Millennials converged. And if there is any reason that management needs to get its act together, it is because Generation Z are nipping at the heels of Millennials.

Their need for speed, innovation, responsiveness, and mobility will make Millennials look like Luddites.

Success for any organization and individual going forward will come to those who are agile enough to adapt quickly, and are adept at simplifying the complexity for others. At this point, management's biggest and scariest problem is exponential change, not the multi-generational workforce. Finding solutions that work will require the contributions, support, and talent of Millennials and Gen Z collaborating with Baby Boomers and older cohorts.

If the acquisition and retention of new young talent is a problem, leadership needs to look in the mirror. A failure to capitalize on abundant opportunity and leverage the talent of nearly 100 million Millennials and Generation Z is the result of poor strategy, hubris, and finger-pointing. Millennials and Generation Z won't be the cause of failure going forward. It will be the failure to challenge the status quo and an inability to adapt fast enough to an exponentially changing environment.

So, next time you consider bashing a Millennial, remember that they didn't cause disruption, but were born into a world when unprecedented economic, demographic and societal shifts occurred. They are simply adapting to the only environment they know.

As Pogo once said, *"We have met the enemy and he is us."*

WHAT COMES AFTER Z?

Meet Generation R.

The real threat to jobs is not China, India, or Asia. It is not Isis or other terrorist groups. It is not the President or Congress. It is not the Millennials or Generation Z. It is Generation R, where

R represents robots. It is a world in which the work is still there but the jobs aren't.

Global economies are already shifting to higher levels of unemployment. Workers need to adjust to the fact that many jobs are disappearing. We also have workers without jobs because they lack necessary skills in fields like medicine, engineering and technology. We have jobs without workers, because too few are willing to work for low pay levels. Both employers and employees need to look at the world of work differently and seek new solutions.

The challenge we face is undeniably and extraordinarily complex and complicated. The conventional approach about work is obsolete. The biggest problem with exponential and accelerating technological change is that it is largely incomprehensible to humans. We are experiencing an unprecedented intellectual renaissance—when computers surpass the human mind in processing power.

How do we make change work for the millions of people who will be unemployable and 45 percent of the current labor force, mostly low-skilled and administrative-dependent workers, who will soon find themselves without jobs?

KEY POINTS

» Stop bashing, mocking, cajoling, and complaining about Millennials.

» Meet Generation Z.

» Embrace Millennials and Gen Z as ambassadors of change and liaisons between the past and future.

QUESTIONS

» What percentage of our workforce will be Millennials and Gen Z in 5 years?

» What percentage of our customers will be Millennials and Gen Z in 5 years?

» What are some of the things we need to learn or change about how we manage Millennials and Gen Z?

» How prepared are we to attract and retain Millennials and Gen Z as employees and customers?

» How will Millennials and Gen Z impact or influence our business strategy?

» What policies will we need to change to adapt to Millennials and Gen Z and how will they impact other generations?

FAVORITE QUOTES ABOUT CHANGE

The only thing that is constant is change.

Heraclitus of Ephesus

Everybody has accepted by now that change is unavoidable. But that still implies that change is like death and taxes—it should be postponed as long as possible and no change would be vastly preferable. But in a period of upheaval, such as the one we are living in, change is the norm.

Peter Drucker, Management Challenges for the 21st Century (1999)

When the winds of change blow, some people build walls and others build windmills.

Chinese Proverb

He who rejects change is the architect of decay. The only human institution which rejects progress is the cemetery.

Harold Wilson

Change your thought and you change your world.

Norman Vincent Peale

If you don't like something, change it. If you can't change it, change your attitude.

Maya Angelou

If you don't like something change it; if you can't change it, change the way you think about it.

Mary Engelbreit

I alone cannot change the world, but I can cast a stone across the waters to create many ripples.

Mother Teresa

I wanted to change the world. But I have found that the only thing one can be sure of changing is oneself.

Aldous Huxley

All great changes are preceded by chaos.

Deepak Chopra

You miss 100% of the shots you never take.

Wayne Gretzy

In a chronically leaking boat, energy devoted to changing vessels is more productive than energy devoted to patching leaks.

Warren Buffett

Change is hard because people overestimate the value of what they have—and underestimate the value of what they may gain by giving that up.

James Belasco and Ralph Stayer, Flight of the Buffalo (1994)

The rate of change is not going to slow down anytime soon. If anything, competition in most industries will probably speed up even more in the next few decades.

John P. Kotter, Leading Change

After living with their dysfunctional behavior for so many years (a sunk cost if ever there was one), people become invested in defending their dysfunctions rather than changing them.

Marshall Goldsmith, Mojo

Your success in life isn't based on your ability to simply change. It is based on your ability to change faster than your competition, customers and business.

Mark Sanborn

Just when I think I have learned the way to love, life changes.

Hugh Prather

You must welcome change as the rule but not as your ruler.

Denis Waitley

If you're in a bad situation, don't worry it'll change. If you're in a good situation, don't worry, it'll change.

John A. Simone, Sr.

There were no violins or warning bells ... no sense that my little life was about to change. But we never know, do we? Life turns on a dime.

Stephen King

The past is the present, and the present the future, to the non-progressive mind.

James Lendall Basford (1845–1915), Sparks from the Philosopher's Stone, 1882

In times of rapid change, experience could be your worst enemy.

J. Paul Getty

Time is a dressmaker specializing in alterations.

Faith Baldwin

Nothing that is can pause or stay;
The moon will wax, the moon will wane,
The mist and cloud will turn to rain,
The rain to mist and cloud again,
Tomorrow be today.

Henry Wadsworth Longfellow

God grant me the serenity to accept the people I cannot change, the courage to change the one I can, and the wisdom to know it's me.

Author Unknown

The greatest danger in times of turbulence is not the turbulence; it is to act with yesterday's logic.

Peter Drucker

Most of our assumptions have outlived their uselessness.

Marshall McLuhan

Never, never, never, never give up.

Winston Churchill

RECRUITING IN THE AGE OF GOOGLIZATION

RECRUITING IN THE AGE OF GOOGLIZATION

A FEW CHAPTERS AGO I wrote, "Most organizations do pretty well at what they do today. It's what they need to be doing tomorrow that is missing." I stand by that statement for getting products out the door and delivering services on time. When it comes to recruiting however I'm not so confident most organizations are meeting expectations right now. In an environment of exponential change, the job is about to get much more difficult.

Employers need to get a grip on reality; viable and practical plans to compete for talent in the current and future workforce are long past due. Management needs to understand where it will find employees to do the work, manage, and run their organizations today, tomorrow, and in the months and years ahead.

For the most part, the recipe for business success will require a masterful blend of recruiting and retaining a diverse and often time global multigenerational workforce while capitalizing on the forces of technology. It will require a lot more creativity than just saying, "People are our most important asset."

Recruiting in the Age of Googlization describes a state where The Art of Recruiting meets the Science of Google. An explanation of recruiting should not be necessary but the meaning of Googlization might not be so obvious.

Googlization is just one part of the much larger shift we are experiencing in the Age of Exponential Change. Google has significantly changed our lives, and I'm not going to argue whether that is good or bad. Gradually, and somewhat insidiously, Google permeates almost everything we do. In response, billions of people have reciprocated and embraced Google. Soon, it might not only dominate our online activities and shape our persona, but transcend into our day-to-day living with autonomous vehicles and virtual reality. It's not only a brand, a product, a multitude of service—it's a verb!

Recruiting did not get a pass—although management and HR often acts like it—when Google decided it was time to put information no further than our fingertips anytime we wanted it. Also, Googlization is not limited to Google and its friendly search box and clever logos. Google as the leader just represents the entirety of a much bigger movement. As Apple did with technology, Google disrupted and then transformed the way the world's people operate, communicate, and interact. Like the genie, Google is out of the bottle and there is no putting it back in. Our lives—including how we seek jobs and find workers—have been forever changed.

It's time to stop resisting, kicking, and fighting change. It's time for companies, and specifically HR, to embrace the world as it is today. Businesses can no longer expect to attract and engage workers if they continue to function as if it were 1970, 1984, or even 2001. Increasingly, Googlization has impacted traditional methods of recruiting to the point where the old ways are dysfunctional, inefficient, and obsolete.

Recruiting in the Age of Googlization is the blueprint to guide you safely through the intersection of Recruiting and Googlization.

Hiring and Recruiting:
Today vs Tomorrow

THE SUCCESS OF YOUR company depends on having a full roster of qualified, competent, and engaged employees to keep every aspect of your business running smoothly. However, according to a recent Jobvite Recruiting Nation Survey,[79] the ability to be fully staffed and productive is getting much harder. Fifty-six percent of recruiters are hurting for skilled or qualified candidates.

In many industries, the problem is much worse. The CEO of the National Association of Home Builders describes the situation as "an epidemic."[80] The Associated General Contractors survey reports 86% of commercial builders are having trouble filling hourly and salaried positions. Sixty-five percent of HR officials at small companies are struggling too.[81] Shortages of skilled labor are starting to drive up costs of building and other projects.

Stories like this pop up in the news on an almost daily basis. It doesn't seem to matter if the company is large or small, urban or rural, product or service oriented, domestic or international. They are representative of three reasons why filling open positions quickly is getting more difficult in the U.S. as well as in many other countries.

Growth: While the economy is not robust, it has been growing at a steady pace and is expected to continue. Many companies are hiring, especially in skilled positions. While this is great news for their companies—and the economy in general—it can be a challenge for hiring managers to fill many positions quickly enough to keep their companies operating efficiently. Going forward, 95% of recruiters expect the hunt for talent to remain or grow more competitive.

Recruiting Options: The growth of the Internet has led to an explosion of recruiting opportunities. Job seekers used to rely on classified ads and word of mouth. Now, they can use job search engines like Indeed, job boards like Craigslist and Monster, social media, online recruitment agencies, and corporate recruiting websites. Nearly 6 out of every 10 employed workers search monthly for a new job[82] … and 65% of new hires look at new jobs again within 91 days of being hired. This at-your-fingertips ability to find new job opportunities has made it ridiculously easy for anyone at any time to submit an application. Consequently, the sheer volume of applications makes it more difficult for companies to screen and vet a high volume of applicants efficiently.

Time: Most recruiters and hiring managers are bombarded with multiple tasks, from placing ads to screening and interviewing potential job candidates. The average recruiter spends from 6 seconds[83] to 4 minutes[84] reading each resume that land on his or her desk, and a minimum of 25 hours each week on the phone sourcing candidates.[85] Because of the high volume of resumes coming in, combined with inadequate applicant management capabilities, the national mean job vacancy duration reached 30.5 days in April 2017[86]—an all-time high and nearly double what it was in January 2010. While attending a recent manufacturing workforce summit, one company shared that 3 years ago it took 30 days to fill an open electro/mechanical technician job; today it takes 130 days. That scenario was reiterated by all 4 panelists. For STEM jobs[87], it takes on average twice as long. For some jobs requiring more advanced skills, 6 months or longer is fairly common. It's a given that even recruiters have only 24 hours in a day and 7 days in a week. Finding more time is not an option.

As you can imagine, there are several business-changing consequences to these trends:

» Too many unqualified applicants congest the hiring process, making it harder to find qualified applicants and extending the duration of job openings.

» When jobs remain unfilled, related tasks are either delegated to inexperienced staff, or not performed at all. As a result, the company's overall productivity and profitability suffers and some companies delay or scale back strategic initiatives.

» Alternatively, some companies feel compelled to hire people who are a poor fit for the job, either temperamentally or professionally. The result is that two-in-five hiring managers attribute a bad hire to pressure to fill the job opening.[88] This pressure to fill an opening with a warm body leads to employee turnover, mistakes and accidents, and overall inefficiency.

How effectively are organizations responding? Not very well. Just take a look at a few of these alarming statistics pulled from the 2017 Annual Recruiting Survey.[89]

» 42% of organizations don't have or don't know if they have a recruiting strategy. Enough said.

» While online recruiting sources such as Monster and CareerBuilder are considered the most successful source by 42% of the organizations surveyed, only 4% agreed they got the "best applicants."

» About 1 in 4 organizations identified the company website as the best source of top talent but nearly 77% stated it played an important or somewhat important role in recruiting.

Despite the almost universality of labor shortages, over 2/3 of companies do not use any software to automate, track, or measure recruiting. The majority of companies aren't using metrics of any kind.

» 74% do not track cost per hire.

» 60% do not measure time-to-fill.

» Nearly 2/3 do not measure quality of hire.

William Edwards Deming once said, *"Without data you're just another person with an opinion."* His words still ring true. Without good data and analytics fixing and improving recruitment will become even more challenging.

To compete effectively going forward, any business must hire (and retain) the most talented people in that industry. That can't be just a goal, but a strategic imperative. That shift in mindset creates a huge problem for many organizations, because conventional practices are no longer good enough to meet recruiting challenges and demands. You can't type a tweet on a typewriter and push it up to the Internet but it doesn't seem to prevent some companies from trying. Familiar but outdated recruiting tools just won't help fill open positions today. Recruitment must be agile, streamlined, and responsive too. The only viable choice is for companies to start recruiting smarter in order to hire faster.

The current marketplace of exponential change and hyper-competitiveness also necessitates that human resources ascend to a more strategic role. Evidence and probability must support each and every decision about sourcing, selection, compensation, and performance management. HR may be headed in the right direction but it sure has a long way to go based on those recent surveys.

R-E-A-C-H More Qualified Applicants

T AKE A STEP BACK in time to the 1950s and imagine yourself as the foreman in a Philadelphia railroad yard. You exit your office, cross the workplace campus, and observe through the fence a gathering mob of job candidates. Like clockwork, a similar crowd greets you each morning.[90] The news about job openings spreads like wildfire through the local neighborhood in these pre-Googlization days. All that separates you and your next hire is a fence. You reach for an orange you carried from the office and loft it over the fence. You invite the lucky guy who caught the orange through the gate entrance, have him sign a few papers, and put him to work. Your whole recruitment strategy and hiring process consists of a handful of oranges and a good throwing arm.

Sourcing and recruiting workers today spins quite a different story. Thanks to technology, the information economy, and social media, job seekers are changing the rules of engagement. Reaching qualified applicants requires a robust strategy significantly more sophisticated than the arm strength of the manager, the hand-eye coordination of the candidate, and an ample supply of fruit.

Just like consumers who have become accustomed to doing online research before purchasing a product or service, job seekers do the same thing. They want to know what it's like to work for you before they apply. They check out your website, and read reviews from customers and employees—current and former. If the company site isn't user-friendly and reviews are unfavorable, applicants can merely swipe their finger across a screen and move on to the next one.

What's a company to do? There are literally thousands of best-recruiting practices available with a quick Google search, but the list can be narrowed down quickly into an acronym I've created. **REACH** equals **R**each—**E**ngage—**A**pply—**C**onverse—**H**ire.

REACH

Job seekers today search for jobs the same way they search for a car, restaurant, or house—they ask their friends for advice, check review sites, and "Google" it. Ninety-one percent of job seekers start their job search and apply for a job using a mobile device[91]. And, on average, they use 18 different sources![92] Depending on a candidate's demographics, skill sets, geography, and a dozen other factors, one person's search might take him to LinkedIn or Twitter and another might lead him to the job search engine, Indeed or a college career fair. Different job categories and locations also might influence where the top talent is hanging out. Finding your next hire will depend on your ability to be seen in the right places at the right times by enough qualified applicants. (There's more on extending the reach in the next chapter.)

ENGAGE

First impressions matter and recruitment is no exception. Guess what happens when an interested candidate clicks to apply, and is turned off by what they see on your career page? Nothing. Nada. Zilch.

The first interaction with a candidate must be interesting, inviting and interactive. A recent study by Dr. John Sullivan and Associates revealed that more than 90% of candidates who reach a company career site do not apply.[93] That's a staggering statistic, and one that would not be tolerated in any other function of business. Boring and transactional career pages are a recruitment killer.

Other studies confirm this atrocious result. For every 100 candidates who click from a job posting to a recruitment portal, only 8 complete the application on a desktop.[94] It's even worse from a mobile device when fewer than 2 candidates who see your posting actually complete an application.[95]

Engagement occurs when a job seeker visits your website, reads online reviews about your company, connects with you and your employees on social media, and still wants to apply. Job posting content needs to motivate the applicant to do more than just click the apply button. It must convert the potential employee from the casual inquirer to an engaged participant. Unfortunately, most company career pages are woefully unappealing—even to the most desperate applicant.

Employment branding is more than a buzzword. The message from candidates is loud and clear: They won't apply simply because you have an opening. They want to know what it's like to work for you and how you treat your employees, your customers, the community, and the environment. In other words, before a company can get the attention of top talent, it has to get its messaging just right ... and walk the talk. Offering a paycheck with benefits is no longer enough. Workers care as much about what the company stands for as the work they will do.[96]

According to a recent survey by Glassdoor, 69% are likely to apply to a job if the employer actively manages its employer brand (e.g., responds to reviews, updates their profile, shares updates on the culture and work environment).[97] On the other hand, 69% would not take a job with a company that had a bad reputation, even if they were unemployed.[98]

It's simple—reputation and presentation matters. Without them, an organization has little to no chance of engaging top talent. Social media and Googlization took branding out of the hands of management and placed it at the feet of the candidate. They can just as easily kick a company to the side as pick you up to play the game. Providing an exceptional first impression as well as nurturing a positive relationship is just as important as offering more pay and benefits. It begins with HR appropriating at least as much attention to the design, content and marketing of talent acquisition as sales and marketing does to customer acquisition.

No candidate should ever be left waiting or wondering, "What's next?" Develop a process for every possible touch point with a candidate and send updates, whether it's an email, phone call, or thank-you note. Whenever a candidate lands on your website, jump at the chance to engage. Some of the process may be automated, but don't ignore the power of the personal chat and phone call, especially for the more qualified applicants.

APPLY

The traditional job application form is a relic from the 1940s. Even with the shift to online recruitment, many organizations merely took the archaic paper application and digitized it, providing little room for companies to distinguish the most skilled and ambitious from the slacker.

The last thing you want to do in a tight job market is make it unpleasant to apply.[99] Qualified candidates leak out of the recruitment funnel at an excruciatingly costly rate.[100] Traditional management and HR thinking hopes that lengthy applications will screen out apathetic candidates and good talent will be dedicated enough to fill out more information. That sounds logical and it used to work—but not in this era.

It's a fact that the majority of organizations struggle to find enough qualified applicants. Most executives place blame on the quality of the labor market. I believe that is only part of the story. Highly effective marketing campaigns entice and engage jobseekers to apply then turn them away with an unfriendly, cumbersome application.

Candidate abandonment is a significant problem. In a study by CareerBuilder, 60% of job seekers quit in the middle of filling out online job applications due to length or complexity. Many companies still require an applicant to email or upload a resume. That is just not a task that many applicants will do using their smartphone, especially for the lower skill/lower pay jobs. Skilled candidates have choices in this tight labor market and are reluctant to submit their resume without some interaction with the company first.

Application length matters too. Applications that take more than 15 minutes[101] to complete experience 365% degradation in completion rates. In other words, 1 out of 7 applicants abandon an application no matter what the length of time required. But over 50% quit when the application has 20 or more questions or takes more than 15 minutes to complete.

So, what can you do to make your job application more appealing and less an impediment to prospective employees?

Start with this question: What information do we absolutely need to know that would automatically disqualify an applicant or identify a potentially good employee?

1. **Identification.** Do you really need the applicant's name at this point? No. Besides, a name just allows unconscious bias to creep in.[102] A phone number or email address is good enough for a candidate to start an application. Having both is convenient, but not essential. All you need is a means to contact the applicant, if he or she is qualified based on his or her responses to the questions.

2. **Education.** Every single one of your questions should help determine if the candidate meets your minimum job requirements. You can simply ask "what is the highest level of education you completed" with a checklist from GED to graduate degree. Isn't this really what you want to know? You can get the names of schools, types of degrees, and dates of graduation later if they meet your minimum requirement.

3. **Experience.** Does the position require a minimum number of years or a specific type of experience? You can simply ask a yes-no question for each one, such as "Do you have a minimum of 5 years' experience?" or provide fill-in-the-blank if you require special skills.

4. **Licenses or Certifications.** Maintain the focus on what you absolutely "need to know." Ask "Do you have a valid license to practice medicine or drive a vehicle?" A simple yes or no does it.

And there you have it, 4 questions that get you exactly what you need to know to disqualify or move forward with an applicant.

Even the best sourcing and engagement strategy falls short when the application process isn't user-friendly. Considerable cost-savings and improvements in completion rates can be achieved when the application uses a "need to know" model.

The bottom line is this: Without the ability to at least start an application on a smartphone or tablet, candidate abandonment is ridiculously high, especially among Millennials and tech-savvy candidates. And if the application is too difficult or too long to complete, job seekers quit the process at a discouragingly high rate. Companies must streamline the way they ask questions, the number of questions they ask, and adapt to the way job seekers want to apply if they expect to REACH more candidates.

CONVERSE

After clicking "submit" on a job application, more than half of applicants sit and wait like abandoned lovers waiting for the phone to ring.[103] Many companies seem to have adopted the foolish practice of "ghosting" when it comes to dealing with job applicants.[104]

What's ghosting, you ask? Ghosting is a new buzzword for the practice of disappearing from a relationship and ignoring texts, phone calls, and other attempts at making contact. *The New York*

Times recently highlighted ghosting in personal relationships[105] but the phenomenon is happening in professional ones, too.

Many employers don't seem to grasp how important communication with candidates is. Eighty-two percent of employers still think that a bad candidate experience has little or no effect on the company.[106] Candidates, the customer in this case, don't see it the same way; 84% of candidates expect a personal email response and more than half anticipate a phone call. Consequently, a majority of employers respond to less than half of the candidates who apply which can partially explain why recruiting top talent is such a challenge. Even fewer do it in a timely manner.

Like the neglected lover, candidates remember when companies don't respond or keep in touch. The same survey shows 58% are less likely to buy from a company if they don't get a response and 69% shun the company after a bad interview experience.

In a world where disappointed candidates can send their bad experience viral with a few keystrokes, it's time for employers to stop mimicking the three wise monkeys who don't see, don't hear, and don't listen. Getting candidates to apply is hard enough, but turning a deaf ear to them after they do is just a horrific practice.[107] Thanking a potential employee for taking the time to apply for job at your company is a small courtesy and a business practice with low investment and high returns. Even the unqualified applicant deserves the courtesy of a response.

You might follow the lead of companies like Salesforce who send candidates "thank you" notes[108] after interviews. A new start-up company, WorkforceIC goes one step further. They suggest clients offer all applicants a discount coupon or free offer after completing its assessment. After all, every applicant is a potential customer too. Besides, who knows who they know that might be a good fit for one of your hard-to-fill positions.

Instead of ignoring applicants, start a conversation. Update them on their application status frequently. Invite them to subscribe to a newsletter, blog or future webinar that keeps them informed about your company, your products, and your opportunities. Like customers, communication is essential to building your brand and sustaining your reputation.

HIRE

Many companies believe the recruiting and selection process ends when "all the paperwork is signed and the employee's first day is complete."[109] Nothing can be further from the truth. One in five final applicants turn down or get cold feet and renege on offers. For those who move forward, many new employees decide to stay or leave within the first three weeks. Twenty-two percent of staff turnover occurs in the first 45 days of employment.[110] Nearly half of all new hires fail in the first 18 months.[111]

To be kind, most onboarding often goes like this: The new hire arrives and the manager introduces him to his cubicle, computer, desk, phone, nearest restroom, and ID badge and extends a hardy 'good luck!' It's sink or swim. Minimalist onboarding helps no one and represents a huge missed opportunity to jumpstart a productive and rewarding relationship. The Aberdeen Group reported that 66% of companies with onboarding programs claimed a higher rate of successful assimilation of new hires into company culture, 62% had higher time-to-productivity ratios, and 54% reported higher employee engagement.[112]

Onboarding offers a compelling proposition. Employees who participate in a structured onboarding process are 58% more likely to be with the organization after three years.[113] Onboarding is as much a part of recruitment process as prospecting for applicants. What good does it do to attract and hire the talent you need only to lose them due to negligence?

The Recruitment ToolKit

No matter how talented your recruiters, marketing department, and human resources staff, their effectiveness is hindered if they don't have the tools and strategy to make screening and hiring processes better.

Use Recruitment Marketing Tools More Effectively

Most companies limit candidate sourcing to ads they post online and in-print media; that's a limiting and guarded approach when talent acquisition requires a more aggressive and concerted marketing plan. For starters, recruitment marketing should include all communications that an organization uses to reach and engage job seekers, from the job posting and personal emails to social media and career fairs. Every company website should provide easy access to a career page. Don't miss opportunities to promote job openings on billing statements and other customer touchpoints. Encourage customers to refer friends and relatives. Employers have dozens of interactions with customers that present opportunities to promote job openings. Few take advantage of them.

It's also past the time when companies should be wondering if social media platforms like Facebook, LinkedIn, Twitter, or

Instagram should be used to promote job openings and careers. The question must be "Which ones should we be using?" To paraphrase an article in Forbes: It's easy to make fun of Facebook. The unguarded vanity of high school "friends" all tends to reinforce the inanity of the social network, but over a billion people use it—even those who complain about it. And for large, multinational companies, it's becoming an increasingly valuable tool for marketing and recruiting employees.[114]And that's just Facebook!

Here's a short list of marketing tools, many of which are free, and available to any size company in any industry.

CAREER SITE

Every company must have its own career site, even if it is only one page. When a job posting is placed only on a third-party site (such as CareerBuilder or Indeed), the marketing opportunity starts and ends when you stop paying, typically 30 days. Within that timeframe, the job posting often slides off the first page or two as new competitor opportunities are posted, unless you invest in sponsored ads. But those too only work as long as you keep funding the meter. A company career site optimized for search engines on the other hand keeps your job posting front and center, 24/7/365.

A company career site provides the opportunity to show off your company and its brand in addition to posting open jobs. It can highlight images of your facility, employee success stories, and provide additional contact details. Make sure to include photos and videos—they bring your culture to life, giving candidates an inside view of what it's like to work there.

JOB POSTING

To grab the attention of a jobseeker, engage him or her with a compelling story. The content must be convincing and motivating. Avoid cutting and pasting the description you use internally. An effective job post should reflect and define your employer brand, and list realistic requirements that attract talent with the right potential rather than scare them away. Don't forget that job titles must be keyword optimized and similar to what candidates will use in their search. Describe your company culture, but be authentic and transparent, not full of rhetoric and buzzwords. Use specific descriptions of required (not just desirable) experience and education and connect them to the job, culture, and overall mission of the company. If a certification, degree, or experience isn't essential, omit it.

SOCIAL MEDIA

To attract enough qualified talent today, effective recruiting requires the intelligent use of social media. Unfortunately, social media is easily abused and misused. Social recruiting also requires the technical skills of marketing, sales, and data science, and the art of conversation all rolled up in one—skill sets many HR professionals haven't acquired. Whether management likes it or not, what other people say about your company is what your brand is, not what you want marketing to say it is. If you don't have company profiles built and optimized for social media channels such as Facebook, LinkedIn, Instagram, and Twitter, other people are doing the talking for you—good and bad. And if they're not talking and sharing, that might be an even bigger problem! If your company and employees are not connected, top talent may question whether your company is an attractive place to work.

How Companies Use Social Media for Employment Branding

» Show off behind-the-scenes of employees going about their daily tasks
» Attract new talent with images of new products, services, and prototypes
» Post pictures of employees with comments about what it's like to work for your company and how long they've been there
» Post photos and stories of happy customers
» Highlight fun things the company does with and for employees
» Showcase how the company helps out the community
» Share inspirational quotes
» Offer tips of the week

A good marketing message is not enough either. Ultimately, consumers and job candidates alike want to know if you really walk the talk. Creating a strategy, maintaining an active presence and regularly publishing contact is a great way to amplify your job openings. Besides, the very best source for talent is still referrals and social media is like word-of-mouth on steroids.

The final word: You don't need to use every social media platform. Pick the one or two that your target demographic uses regularly. For young frontline and staff workers, it might be Facebook and Instagram. For professionals, sales, and management, LinkedIn has become a virtual Rolodex. Twitter is a quirky tool but highly effective in certain geographic areas and industries.

BLOG

Blogging isn't just for techies, foodies, and political junkies. A blog provides an inexpensive, but powerful way to build your employment brand and raise awareness. Start a blog to showcase who you are and what you stand for. Attract candidates with relevant how-to career articles and posts about what it's like to work for your company. Include tips about how to prepare for an interview and improve career skills. Encourage employees to write articles about their careers, working at your company, and even where and how they volunteer. Feature company news and employee success stories too. Don't hesitate to offer advice for professional and personal development, even if it's not related specifically to your company. You might even consider department or job-specific blogs (such as tech or sales) for hard-to-fill positions.

VIDEO

Speaking about video ... video isn't really a stand-alone recruitment tool but its importance is growing so rapidly, it deserves to be highlighted. It's a must-have on your company career page, social media campaigns, blogs and newsletters. To be fair video alone won't fill all those open positions but attracting enough applicants without it will be next to impossible—for no other reason than Google loves video. Moovly Media and Forrester Research reports video is more than 50 times more likely to show up first on Google. Given the choice between video and text, an overwhelmingly majority of consumers prefer video. Why has video become so popular? It's mobile friendly. It can be watched on nearly every platform, from the smartphone to TV.

While many job boards don't allow the placement of video, company career sites do. Video is no longer just a nice touch—it's an essential strategy. In fact, videos drive traffic better than any other single form of content. Social media loves video too.

Here's some good news too. While professionally produced videos have their place, shorter and more authentic videos are even more effective. How short? 15 seconds to 1 minutes max! How authentic? Even personal smartphones now capture high resolution images and you can't get more authentic than that. While professionalism is important, don't be afraid to post "YouTube" quality videos and even selfies. Other effective video strategies include a brief introduction from managers and "a day in the life" at your company. They appeal to the modern-day candidate seeking authenticity, not promotional hype.

Whether it's a 30 second interview with a current employee, a quick tour of your facility, or just a brief announcement about a job opening, video is an affordable, highly effective way to "humanize" your company.

EVENTS

Who said that face-to-face communication is dead? Despite the perception that Millennials only text and "selfie," surveys confirm that they value face-to-face meetings as much as, if not more than, other generations. However, events take time and money. While college job fairs and other networking events are still effective, they are not always practical. Online events are growing in popularity. They are affordable and as simple as scheduling a webinar or conference call on Skype or Google Hangout. Announce job openings to participants during a scheduled webinar, and then have an open discussion about the job, what it's like to work at the company, or just open it up for questions. Schedule some time each week to answer questions posted by candidates on sites like Quora or within LinkedIn groups.

EMAIL MARKETING

Believe it or not, email can be effective. Emails continue to be read by many people from every generation—even Millennials, particularly when the content is targeted to them. Create emails that inspire, engage, and delight both passive and active candidates. While personalized messages are preferred, tasteful automated ones work too. As for definite no-no's: Do not blast out emails with generic messages that reek of advertising, as they will likely be deleted or identified as spam. They may even do more harm than good. Email marketing requires informative, useful, and engaging content to a targeted audience.

TEXT MESSAGES (SMS)

Text messages may be the 21st century version of the classified ad. And with 80% of smartphone users checking their devices 150+ times each day and opening text messages 99% of the time, using text to source and recruit candidates presents a pretty compelling argument. Text can work at any stage of the recruiting funnel too. Companies can text prospects to gauge interest or follow-up with them to provide updates or reminders, schedule interviews, or request additional information. With so many candidates already working other jobs, connecting by phone often leads to extended games of voice message tag. Some local businesses are finding geographic-targeted messages are a simple and effective way to let people passing by that your company has a job opening. This is extremely effective for retail, hospitality, restaurants, and healthcare. Texting offers a more convenient platform from which to conduct an initial screen too. Texting however should be used with some caution. Acceptance of texting for recruiting has greater engagement with Millennials and Gen Z than older workers who may view it as unprofessional. As with any recruiting tactic and tool, it pays to understand your labor market and candidates' preferences.

OLD SCHOOL TOOLS

The purpose of recruiting is to fill open positions as quickly as possible with the highest quality candidate. Turnover and new job creation opens up opportunity all the time so it makes sense to avoid recreating the wheel each time. The recruiting tools mentioned above allow an organization to build a talent pipeline, an engaged database of qualified candidates from which recruiters can continuously pull candidates.

However, let's not forget about opportunities available through some traditional recruiting sources and strategies that can be improved by tweaking them a bit.

CLASSIFIED ADS

While traditional newspapers are going the way of dinosaurs, classified ads in community and local newspapers are still a good way to get the word out. But classified ads, especially print ads, take more time to get published and get noticed. Classifieds may also be helpful in certain industries when well-read publications or association websites reach the highly skilled specialized candidate. They typically cost more, deliver lower ROI, and do not produce consistently good results. But depending upon the job, industry, and the community in which you recruit, classified ads can still work. Many high-traffic areas like grocery stores and restaurants provide bulletin boards that allow employers to post flyers. Whether it's an ad, flyer, or door hanger, these approaches take a shotgun-like approach to advertising rather than a more effective targeted strategy.

JOB BOARDS

Monster, Careerbuilder, and Indeed are still popular and allow recruiters to post ads in searchable databases that are seen by people all over the country as well as around the world. These sites are often flooded with spam ads, however, making it harder for job seekers to find your ads. Some employers opt to pay a fee to search a job board's database. Like the applications you receive by email, it's just as likely that many of the candidates in the database are not qualified. A jobseeker's application padded with the right key words has a better chance of landing a Pulitzer Prize than guaranteeing he can do the job. The process is equivalent to finding the proverbial needle in the haystack, a tactic that requires a lot of time and resources – two assets in short supply these days.

Internal job boards

Promoting internal candidates is one of the most effective means of recruiting, especially when a company has invested successfully in extensive workforce planning and succession management. Internal job boards enable you to recruit from within your organization, allowing current employees to apply before anyone else does. Since these candidates are already familiar with your organization, the orientation time is drastically shorter. A disadvantage of posting internally may be a smaller pool—familiarity with the business isn't the same as understanding the job.

Key Points

1. Multiple sourcing and recruiting options can help attract more candidates by:

   » Expanding the pool of potential candidates, both in terms of numbers and geographic location;

   » Slashing advertising costs through free and low-cost listing sites;

   » Allowing ads to go viral through content marketing and social media;

   » Reaching both passive and active job seekers.

2. But too many sources can also stifle or even cripple an organization when:

   » Campaigns attract a higher volume of resumes, making screening more time-consuming and difficult;

   » Manual-time-intensive processes can't filter out candidates who lack basic qualifications;

   » Poor tracking and a lack of analytics can't link the best applicants to a specific sourcing channel.

Optimize! Become "Mad-Men" of Recruiting

I N A SEARCH-DRIVEN digital world, recruiting tools like those just described are merely commodities—available to anyone who wants to use them. A level playing field doesn't mean the tools can't be effective. What differentiates one company from the next, and one campaign from the next is how effectively job content is optimized and how effective HR can think like "mad-men" marketers.

Unfortunately, for as long as anyone can remember, marketing and HR have coexisted like oil and water. Today, they must blend together like sugar and spice. It's time for HR, especially recruiters, to adopt a marketing mindset and partner with marketing departments and professionals to REACH more applicants. When it comes to online marketing, HR is woefully behind.

Here's one example of the major disconnect: When a company decides to advertise for a job, HR typically reaches for its job description and performs a copy and paste. The job description may be legally compliant, but functionally useless for marketing. It often contains few if any searchable keywords. With more than 9 out of every 10 job searches being started by an online search, employers can't afford to ignore the impact of poor search-engine optimization.

A candidate often begins his job search with a few keywords, typically a job title. Sometimes he might search for a company name. Other times, it could be a specific skill or location. Whatever words or phrases he types must be the same words you include in the company's job title and posting. Unfortunately, that's not often the case. Without the right keywords and content, the chances of qualified candidates finding your job opportunity are slim to none. Just like searches for anything from restaurants to headline news, getting your job posting to show up on the top of first page is critical to attracting more applicants.

The first milestone of any recruitment campaign then is to increase visibility of the job posting. If applicants don't know you have a job opening, they can't apply. Consequently, to reach and attract more applicants, marketing content must be laced within the fabric of recruiting. Obviously, if every competitor is using the same job titles and job descriptions, there must be more reasons why some job postings reach number one and others are buried several pages down the list. Here are a few basic tips for writing online job postings that get noticed.

SEO

HR has more than its share of acronyms, such as EEO, ADA, and FMLA. It's time to add SEO to its lexicon. SEO stands for Search Engine Optimization. Of course, you might be thinking "what the heck does SEO have to do with HR? Isn't that a function of online marketers and website developers?" Yes, of course it is, but recruiting today is as much marketing as it is HR. SEO is a make-or-break ingredient of every recruiting campaign. To get noticed by job applicants more often and more quickly, job titles and job descriptions must be search engine optimized and that includes applying the same best practices that digital marketers use on the company's product landing pages. With over 300 million job-related searches just on Google each month and more than 24,000 gigabytes of data uploaded to the Internet every second, it is all too easy for your job posting to become an insignificant and invisible blip in a sea of information.

Do Research First

Keywords are like cookie crumbs; they lead an applicant to your treasure. Whatever words or phrases an applicant is typing are the same words or phrases that a recruiter should be using in the job posting. Google offers a free AdWords tool called Keyword Planner. Even if you don't plan to promote your jobs using AdWords, the tool still suggests the most popular keywords used in search engines and the difficulty you'll face when it comes to outranking competitors. Google Trends is another free tool to tell you what interest there is around a keyword along with suggestions for similar words. You can also just use Google's autocomplete function that reveals a list of suggestions based on the job title you type into its search box. Search, too, for jobs using different variations of titles on job boards like Monster, CareerBuilder, and Indeed. What jobs show up on top? What words did competitors use to rank number one in job searches? Include those keywords in your job titles and ad copy to increase chances that the people you're looking for will see your job posting.

Use Simple, Search-Friendly Job Titles

Creative job titles are fun and engaging within a company culture, but not so good for recruiting. Stick to variations of familiar titles commonly used in your industry. Director of First Impression might look great on a business card and desk placard but when desperate to find a receptionist, it's best to use the words jobseekers search such as receptionist, secretary, or administrative assistant. One client recently complained to me he wasn't receiving enough applications for HVAC technician openings. I searched for his job posting and couldn't find it. When I asked the job title he used, he replied, "Comfort Care Technician." Sure enough, it showed up number one when I searched again but I'll bet my last dollar that not too many HVAC technicians are searching for Comfort Care Technician jobs. Sometimes it's best to just call it like it is and invest in optimizing the content of your job posting. Some companies find success by including a brand name or other descriptor in the job title such as Apple Retail Salesperson or Home & Bath Customer Service Representative.

OPTIMIZE YOUR CONTENT

Since nearly every competitor will be using similar job titles, search engine optimized content will be the difference between your job posting showing up on the first page verses the last. To figure out what's working and to get those creative juices flowing, pay attention to competitive job postings that show up first. Did they include a lot of copy or were they short and to the point? Were images, video, or bullets used? Was the writing style business-like or fun and casual? Don't limit your search to just your job titles. Pick any popular job title and search for the job. What's working in other industries? Be creative. Searching outside your industry may be what it takes to give you the edge. Whatever you do, don't copy-and-paste your standard job description. It just doesn't work. Make sure you repeat the job title several times in the body of the content. In the HVAC posting I mentioned earlier, the recruiter never used the phrase "HVAC technician." As the idiom goes, "if you don't ask, you won't receive." Use bullet points instead of full sentences and long paragraphs to make the description easy to read. Does your company have or sell a recognizable brand? Use it. Are abbreviations such as RN for Registered Nurse common in your industry? Include them too. And don't forget to add your city and state because many job searches are local.

BE SPECIFIC

If a job description is too vague, you will likely make more work for yourself. You will receive applications and resumes from people who are either unqualified for the job or wouldn't be interested in doing it even if accepted. To better match tasks to talent, write short detailed ads with better descriptions (including key search terms described above) of the requirements and tasks. A rule of thumb is to keep your job posting under 500 words. That means the content must be engaging and succinct to appeal to qualified applicants but specific enough to discourage ill-fitted candidates from applying.

ADD A CODE TO EACH AD

In a perfect world, every company should have a comprehensive analytics system to measure the response to each ad, social media post, and link. But even without that, you can still get a basic breakdown of how well each ad is performing. Assign a unique code to each ad and ask applicants to include it with their applications. This gives you at least a general idea of which ads are working. Most applicant processing software (APS)—also called applicant tracking software—automatically assigns a unique code. If you're not using an APS, adding a code or creating a unique URL is fairly easy to do or ask your web developer to help.

1970 Called ...
It Wants Its Recruiting Model Back

TRUTH BE TOLD, many companies today still manage recruiting as their grandparents did. They spend an inordinate amount of time on administrative tasks such as opening emails then sorting, screening, and filing resumes and applications. Playing phone tag with applicants to schedule screening calls is a whole other time and resource intensive adventure. Long after a recruitment campaign has ended, a few organizations may conduct a "post-mortem" review to determine what went wrong. Most organizations still rely on the spreadsheet to report their success or failure, costs to hire, and other metrics. That, too, takes time—a precious commodity in short supply especially when another manager impatiently waits for his open positions to be filled.

Delays in filling job vacancies are expensive. Costs associated with hiring are climbing in part to these delays. A key performance indicator (KPIs) for a recruiter these days therefore must be time-to-fill *as well as* the quality-of-hire. To track KPIs and make critical adjustments on the fly require real-time data, not the weeks- or months-old documentation commonly collected and later entered in spreadsheets.

Without some automation, data collection and entry takes time which paradoxically takes recruiters away from working directly with candidates. With an increasing demand for speed and accuracy, recruiters and hiring managers must invest their time on business functions that matter, not "busy-ness." Administrative tasks that don't require complex decision making or problem-solving should be reassigned. At one time that meant hiring an assistant. Today these time-intensive administrative-type tasks can be automated.

Recruiting automation is often associated with software that can broadcast job postings to dozens of sources with just a few keystrokes. Dozens of hours can be saved by avoiding the time intensive task of reentering and posting a job opening to multiple sources. The real value however, and one that is overlooked by many people, is that many recruiting software platforms provide access to real-time metrics. With metrics a company can assess what's working and what's not as it happens. Ineffective job postings can be identified and adjusted right away. It makes no sense to have to wait weeks or months for a post-campaign report to figure out what could be done differently. Recruiters should have at their fingertips metrics such as how many people viewed a job post, then started to apply vs completed an application any time they choose. Metrics like ROI per source and quality of hire shouldn't be complicated to compute or cumbersome to access. (You'll read about these recruiting metrics and more in the coming pages.)

Because labor market conditions are increasingly competitive, dynamic and unpredictable, fighting the war for talent with yesterday's data is like entering a gun fight with a knife.

Organizations need every edge they can get to attract talent and fill open positions quickly. There is only one benefit for recruiters to keep recruiting the way they've always done it—job security.

Whatever the recruitment strategy you use, automated or not, data on candidates will come from multiple sources and multiple people. Each candidate's record includes dozens, if not hundreds, of data points—from name and address to performance evaluations. Resumes, applications, and personnel records contain what data science calls structured data—information that is easily formatted. Unfortunately, quite a bit of critical HR data is neither structured nor clean.

Employee data in many organizations might be strewn across a manager's desk or stuffed in HR filing cabinets. Even technology doesn't help when the data is spread out over several software systems from recruiting software to payroll. The end result is lots of information protected by departmental silos and bureaucratic inefficiency filed away with no semblance of order or logic.

What makes it even more challenging is that much of the data that contains the hidden gems is collected as free form text. What do you do with a manager's handwritten comments made during an interview or following a performance reviews? How do you digitize them into a format that can be used and analyzed? Unstructured data is the bane of people analytics.

Thanks to inaccessible and unstructured data, most organizations can't find the best talent when they need it even when that person sits right under a recruiter's or manager's nose. Each job vacancy begins a new campaign and the recruitment wheel spins again. This is inefficient, time consuming, and a colossal waste of money.

Nearly every business function has opened their doors to technology to help manage and predict performance better. Why has HR been granted an exception? It's time for HR to get on the bandwagon.

An excellent starting point for companies struggling with recruitment and attrition is utilization of Applicant Processing Software (APS), often called Applicant Tracking System (ATS). Associated fees have plummeted and often cost much less than current monthly company expenditures on sponsored job posts, staffing agencies, and outside recruiters not to mention savings from efficiency and increased productivity. The right APS leverages automation to replace low value administrative tasks and allow recruiters and hiring managers to focus on the mission critical aspects of employee selection—interviewing and testing qualified candidates.

Equally important to how an APS manages sourcing and screening is its reporting function. The right system provides one-click reports detailing the source of each candidate, the effectiveness of each source and just-in-time analysis of what's working and what's not. It allows you to capture information that leads to cost-to-hire and quality-of-hire too.

Here are a few more key benefits that come from automated recruiting and screening.

FASTER RECRUITING

Think about all the time you spend gathering resumes and cover letters, reviewing them, and organizing them into categories that help you weed out the most (and least) qualified candidates. With time-to-hire at an all-time high and internal resources strained, automation is a strategic necessity. The right APS can screen and sort qualified from unqualified candidates with several keystrokes, saving hundreds of hours of processing paperwork, exchanging unnecessary voice mail and emails, and wasting time interviewing unqualified candidates. Time saved using Applicant Processing Software is time better spent on seeking the best sourcing channels and investing more quality time with high potential candidates. Anything that shortens the time required to fill an open position returns big dividends to the bottom line.

HIGHER PRODUCTIVITY

Low-level but time-intensive administrative functions only drag out the process and add unnecessary costs. It is not unusual for HR managers to hire additional staff to collect and organize their records, but those costs add up over time. Plus, even those workers can be put to better use if they're handling more important tasks in the recruiting process. An effective hiring system ensures that job openings are filled quickly with quality hires with a minimum of wasted time and resources.

MORE TIME WITH QUALIFIED APPLICANTS

The time most recruiters spend on each resume and application is far too short to make informed decisions and be confident that the chosen candidate is right for the job. With applicant processing software helping to collect, organize, and mine applicant data, qualified candidates float to the surface much more quickly. Recruiters can then focus and take time to scour and scrutinize candidates most likely to succeed.

Lower Costs

At first glance, an applicant processing system might seem like yet another expense that your organization can't afford. But look over the benefits listed above; they all lead to greater returns on investment. Posting multiple jobs to multiple job sites takes time. Each site has different posting logins, posting mechanisms, and different requirements. With a single login and simultaneous posting to dozens of job boards with one click, an APS saves time per hire. Many systems also include free or discounted posting on some of the most popular job boards including Indeed, Monster, and CareerBuilder. Building and updating a company career page is time consuming but most APS include a custom page that automatically updates your job openings for free. An APS enables you to collect all the applications in one place, track their progress, schedule interviews and automate a lot of communication that might otherwise have to be done manually. None of those features holds a candle to the cost-saving benefits of improved compliance, real-time reporting, and the ability to build a talent pipeline that shorten time-to-hire.

Not a Magic Bullet

The decision to purchase recruiting software shouldn't be made out of desperation and neither management nor recruiters should expect miracles. Like any purchase, be realistic and define clear expectations. Perform due diligence, but realize a long evaluation and decision process may be a waste of time, too, because advancements in technology change the software almost daily. Often times it's not the software that makes a difference as much as the support and service your vendor provides.

While automation will ultimately be a critical component of any recruiting process, it's not the magic bullet either. Technology undoubtedly improves productivity but it also disrupts how things get done. That's not a bad thing. It's just a fact. When implementations fail, the cause can often be traced back to a change in work flow or individual recruiter habits and not the software itself. The better you plan and the smoother the implementation, the quicker you will see results.

Whether you're choosing an Applicant Processing System for the first time or looking to get more value from the one you have, keep these things in mind.

YOU STILL NEED PEOPLE.

Applicant Processing Systems, like all other forms of automation, threaten employees. Many fear the software will take away their jobs. That may be true in the future, particularly when an APS is enhanced with artificial intelligence and machine learning. But for now, an APS just eliminates many of the administrative tasks and allows the recruiter to focus on candidate engagement, conducting better interviews with the most qualified applicants, and analyzing the strengths and merits of each candidate. Recruitment is still a relationship business and it requires people, especially to nurture positive relationships and reach passive candidates.

GET PEOPLE INVOLVED.

Every business has that one person who refuses to change. They prefer the old way of doing things and they hate the changes around them. That person's stubbornness can hold back the entire organization, because everyone else has to accommodate his refusal to adapt. However, waiting for people to catch up on the skills required to do what's needed ends badly for most companies. Engage stakeholders before you purchase the system. They do the job every day and understand the work flow. Getting users involved in the buying decision always makes implementation easier.

TRAINING IS ESSENTIAL.

It takes time to learn a new system. Be practical, but don't shortcut the time it takes employees to become comfortable with a new way of doing things. Most people are more than capable of learning how to use an APS. (If they're not, that's another issue you'll need to deal with.) It's the change in workflow going from paper to digital or changing from one software program to another that throws a wrench into most implementations. Discuss the workflow step-by-step—what will change from the way things are done now compared to after the system is functional. Once in place, provide a support system that helps users resolve last-minute kinks or get quick refreshers on basic tasks. Be diligent about breaking users of old habits and transitioning them to the new system as soon as possible. And be sure you have managers ready to hold laggards accountable.

DON'T OVERBUY.

For many companies, the temptation is to purchase a system with lots of bells and whistles. Don't do that! You will likely pay for more than you need, and by the time you're ready to use more advanced features, new updates will be required, technology will change, or new competitors will become available. Features you don't plan to use right away also impede training and implementation. As with any software, many of the available features are nice to have, but rarely, if ever, used. Just think about one of the most popular software systems in the world—Microsoft Office. How many people really use all the programs included or the advanced functions? Identify your goals and purchase accordingly.

SUMMARY

The state of recruiting is at a crossroads. Organizations need to rethink how they recruit in the Age of Googlization. The number of recruiting channels has exploded. The new economy has flooded talent pipelines with record levels of unemployed, underemployed, and disengaged workers. This has led to an explosion of resumes and applications, which has essentially overwhelmed the time and resources available to recruiters, hiring managers, and HR. It has forced recruiters to cut the time they dedicate to each candidate when due diligence is more important than ever before.

Jeff Hoffman, co-founder of Priceline and billionaire entrepreneur, shared a great tip with me (along with about 100 other attendees at a summit) last year that holds significant relevance for recruitment. Hoffman recommends an exercise he calls "info-sponging."

He spends up to 20 minutes a day reading something that has nothing to do with his business or what he does. It could be a newspaper, a book, website, or a magazine article. Info-sponging forces you to look outside your industry for innovative solutions.

He points to business disruptors that supposedly came out of nowhere. The idea of the fast-food drive-thru window came from banks. The music industry blew off the MP3 so Apple invented iTunes. Uber was not created by a taxi company and Airbnb didn't come out of the hotel industry. Netflix isn't the genius idea of the movie industry either. Incremental improvement might come from competitors but solutions will likely come from outside-in. Management and HR needs to start info-sponging and learn from organizations outside their community and industry.

Automating administrative functions such as job postings, pre-screening, and sending emails is also strategically essential. Companies that automate experience lower recruiting costs, faster hiring, better quality of hires, and a more productive workforce. If your company wants to stay competitive, upgrade your REACH, focus on a better candidate experience, and arm your HR team with an automated tracking system. Before you know it, you'll be screening faster and hiring smarter, too.

KEY POINTS

» Filling open positions quickly is getting more difficult in the U.S. as well as many other countries.

» While it's easy to point fingers at a shortage of skilled labor, the blame for a lack of qualified applicants often falls squarely on the shoulders of management and recruiters.

» Best recruitment practices require that organizations automate routine and repetitive tasks such as posting jobs, building communities with social media, and responding to candidates quickly and often.

QUESTIONS

» How many applicants need to view our job postings to secure a good pool of candidates?

» Which social media platforms are most effective at referring the most qualified applicants for each job in our company?

» How many applicants start and then complete our application?

» What are the sources that produce the highest quality of hire?

» What is our cost of acquisition by source?

» What is our time to hire by source?

» What is our attrition by source?

» What is our attrition by manager?

FAVORITE QUOTES ABOUT RECRUITING

I hire people brighter than me and I get out of their way.

Lee Iacocca

The competition to hire the best will increase in the years ahead. Companies that give extra flexibility to their employees will have the edge in this area.

Bill Gates

The secret of my success is that we have gone to exceptional lengths to hire the best people in the world.

Steve Jobs

A company should limit its growth based on its ability to attract enough of the right people.

Jim Collins

Some people can do one thing magnificently, like Michelangelo, and others make things like semiconductors or build 747 airplanes—that type of work requires legions of people. In order to do things well, that can't be done by one person, you must find extraordinary people.

Steve Jobs

Get the right people on the bus and the wrong people off the bus.

Jim Collins

We do not hire experts neither do we hire men on past experiences or for any position other than the lowest. Since we do not take a man on his past history, we do not refuse him because of his past history. I never met a man who was thoroughly bad. There is always some good in him if he gets a chance.

Henry Ford

Hire character. Train skill.

Peter Schutz

If you can hire people whose passion intersects with the job, they won't require any supervision at all. They will manage themselves better than anyone could ever manage them. Their fire comes from within, not from without. Their motivation is internal, not external.

Stephen Covey

A great person attracts great people and knows how to hold them together.

Johann Wolfgang Von Goethe

The smartest business decision you can make is to hire qualified people. Bringing the right people on board saves you thousands, and your business will run smoothly and efficiently.

Brian Tracy

As a business owner or manager, you know that hiring the wrong person is the most costly mistake you can make.

Brian Tracy

Recently, I was asked if I was going to fire an employee who made a mistake that cost the company $600,000. No, I replied, I just spent $600,000 training him. Why would I want somebody to hire his experience?

Thomas John Watson Sr.

I am convinced that nothing we do is more important than hiring and developing people. At the end of the day you bet on people, not on strategies.

Lawrence Bossidy

If you think it's expensive to hire a professional to do the job, wait until you hire an amateur.

Red Adair

If you pay peanuts, you get monkeys.

Chinese Proverb

PEOPLE ANALYTICS

What's Next for HR?

CAN YOU IMAGINE what it would be like to travel back in time to the early 1900s and explain to a friend what a smartphone is?

Friend:	"What's that tool you're holding in your hand?"
You:	"That's not a tool. It's my smartphone."
Friend:	"What does it do? How does it work?"
You:	"You just touch the screen and you can access all sorts of information."
Friend:	"What kind of information?"
You:	"Anything I want—news, music, movie times, answers to questions. I can even check my bank account balances, learn how to play the guitar, find a new job, or get ink stains out of my favorite shirt."
Friend:	"What else can it do?"
You:	"I can call friends and clients by just speaking their names."
Friend:	"Without calling an operator or dialing?"
You:	"Yes, and you can even text a message or send an email."
Friend:	"Ok, please slow down. I have a lot of questions. What's a text and an email and where does the information come from?"
You:	"It comes from the Internet?"
Friend:	"What's the Internet?"

Okay, you probably get the idea that a lot of things that we take for granted would simply dazzle anyone born 100 or more years ago. Sitting there inside your time machine, you just want to tell them how much this invention will change the world, but they look at you as if you have two heads. Can you blame them?

Even today it's a bit mind-boggling to think about what a sophisticated device the smartphone is. Nestled neatly inside the cover is one trillion times more processing than the most powerful computer in 1956 and more than all that NASA had back in 1969 when it placed two astronauts on the moon. Working quietly behind the screen is a 3-axis gyroscope, 3-axis magnetometer, accelerometer, GPS, humidity sensor, temperature sensor, pressure sensor, and proximity sensor to name just a few of the high-tech functions that make a smartphone do what it does. And I didn't even mention the camera and microphone! While we still call it a "phone," making calls is likely the simplest function it performs (and the one least used by Millennials and Generation Z).

How soon will it be until we take robots, sensors, and artificial intelligence for granted too? Just as the smartphone revolutionized the way we communicate, these revolutionary technologies are changing the way work gets done. They're changing how candidates seek jobs and how companies source, screen, select, and hire workers. Human resources is looking less conventional and more like science fiction with each passing day.

Let me take you for a little ride into the very near future. Jump in, and buckle up.

Imagine you're a forklift operator applying for a new job. You click on the "Apply Now" button. A next generation artificial intelligence personal assistant, such as Siri or Alexa, responds thanking you for your application. It engages you in a preliminary, very human-like conversation and proceeds to ask you a few screening questions.

"Congratulations," it says. "I think you might be a good fit for our company. Let's get you scheduled to meet with our team." It then offers you several appointment times for an interview. You select one, and a confirmation with directions and instructions is texted to you right away.

When you arrive for the interview, you are greeted by a very friendly, human-looking robot. Now you might be put off by this type of man-and-machine interaction, but it's all part of a sophisticated and predictive screening process. The company is testing to see how you interact with technology, since collaboration with machines is an integral part of its culture.

The robot invites you to follow it through the door and down the corridor. You enter a room filled with a small conference desk and chairs on one side and a device that looks like a forklift in the corner.

"Please climb into the cab of the forklift simulator," the robot tells you. "Watch your step."

As you settle in, an exact replica of the company warehouse floor plan appears on the screen in front of you.

The video starts and your pre-employment test has begun. Your body language, heart rate, blood pressure, respiration rate, and even your eye movements are being monitored as you find yourself driving down a long aisle with three-story-high shelving on either side.

You notice a box teetering on the edge of a shelf just ahead. As you approach, it begins to fall off the shelf, and you swerve and avoid hitting it. You continue, confident that you just averted an accident.

A few seconds later, a co-worker steps out of an aisle without looking. You brake immediately and avoid hitting him too. You're feeling good because you've just avoided a serious workplace injury.

The simulation continues for about five minutes as you successfully maneuver past each obstacle. The video ends and you anticipate that you passed the test with flying colors. You weren't involved in a single mishap and you didn't damage any products or structure. The robot asks you to step down and escorts you into another room. The hiring manager seated at the table asks you to take a seat.

Without hesitation he says, "I'm sorry to tell you that you didn't pass the test." How can that be? You avoided every falling object and obstacle. You should have had a perfect score.

As it turns out, your stellar gaming skills might help you win a few games playing against your buddies, but they don't count so much when the company cares more about your ability to anticipate and avoid risk, not just escape it.

Thanks to advancements in artificial intelligence, facial and eye recognition technology, and virtual reality, the scenario I just outlined is all possible today. Software can now track eye movements as well as monitor your body functions. Think Fitbit on steroids. Where were you looking right before the box fell or the co-worker darted out in front of the forklift? Were you actively scanning and surveying the environment? Isn't that what an employer really wants to know—if the applicant is cautious as well as responsive?

Technologies like this are right on the cusp of disrupting the whole employee screening and selection process, particularly in the area of pre-employment testing and applicant processing software. Simulations won't just assess technical ability but also leadership potential, problem-solving abilities, selling skills, and customer service orientation.

Advanced technologies will immerse the applicant in a virtual reality where skills, abilities, and knowledge will be assessed while the candidate engages in real-life work scenarios. And, like the forklift example, applicants won't be tested on gaming ability and personality preferences, but on real life responses and abilities.

That's just the tip of the iceberg. Once all the data has been captured from the recruiting software, hiring manager, references, and pre-employment testing, you call your artificial intelligence assistant, Alexa, to spin the data and predict the candidate's future success.

"Alexa, whom should I hire?" you ask.

Alexa responds.[115] "I expect Robert to be an excellent fit for your company," she continues. "Robert will be 82% engaged after 90 days and demonstrate insignificant flight risk for 42 months. He will perform best on teams managed by Susan A. But if paired with Jim, his performance rating declines to 79% and flight risk is under 2 years; with Alice, success drops to 64%."

You might be thinking this type of scenario reeks of science fiction and futurism. You would be wrong. The future isn't coming; it's here today. Alexa and other AI assistants represent the convergence of big data, AI, and machine learning. As a result, the demand for better people outcomes is exploding and HR is caught in its downdraft. Management demands a crystal ball, but

HR responds so far with a rear-view mirror.

Welcome to the new world of work where reality seems to be leaping off the pages of science fiction right into our everyday experiences! It's not a matter of *if* but *when* artificial intelligence, sensors, machine learning, and robots are going to disrupt every aspect of work and change how people apply for work, get hired, and are managed.

While the number of organizations that have achieved Alexa-like outcomes is small, the pursuit of this level of sophistication and predictability is hot. People analytics have swung past the tipping point of a buzzword to an essential business intelligence service. The number of companies using analytics to make better decisions about talent acquisition and people management will explode in the next few years.

Is Technology Making
Pre-Employment Testing Obsolete?

Before moving onto highly advanced analytics, let's step back a minute to see how we got here in the first place.

For nearly 100 years, employers have been testing job applicants to make sure they were a good fit. An applicant completed a questionnaire and the employer received a report describing his personality, job fit, skills, and abilities. Utilization of these pre-employment tests skyrocketed in the 80s and 90s thanks to computerization and again more recently when most assessments were re-coded for the "cloud."

Technology has made pre-employment testing employer-user friendly. No longer are the services of an industrial or organizational psychologist required to administer and interpret results. Getting the results often took days if not weeks. Fees for a single test and interpretation often reached $2,500 which made it cost prohibitive except for a few executive positions. Today, computers run by sophisticated algorithms analyze an applicant's responses in real time and deliver detailed reports to recruiters in seconds. Many test publishers write user-friendly profile reports for the recruiter or manager, not a psychologist or other assessment professional. Algorithms are slowly replacing the tasks that many professionals performed and are democratizing the services they render.

What hasn't changed much is the format of the testing. Technology has enhanced delivery and algorithms improved accuracy. Unfortunately, the candidate experience is pretty much the same. Candidates complete a questionnaire that includes anywhere from 20 questions to several hundred. The only difference is they might use a mobile device or personal computer instead of paper and pencil. The questionnaires themselves haven't changed much over time.

That is until now. Psychologists have squeezed traditional testing as far as it can go. With the stakes for making the right hiring decision and avoiding mistakes higher than ever, it is my prediction that as early as 2022 new technological advancements will completely disrupt the pre-employment test industry. The traditional pre-employment test as we know it will become as useful as using a typewriter to search the Internet. Assessment providers will be forced to change both the construction and delivery of employee tests to deliver better predictive results and provide user-friendly experiences.

Watch out for significant advancement in the field of pre-hire assessments over the next 5 to 10 years driven by these three factors:

1. **Predictive Analytics.** Moving forward, the employment testing industry will be disrupted by advancements in technologies and tools such as artificial intelligence and data mining. Testing applicants and employees will shift from an "active" model to "passive." Passive assessments will not look like tests at all and will have a very low impact on

job applicants' time and attention. In the passive model, a profile will be collected from data using ongoing interactions by and with candidates—much like the retailers collect data from consumers.

2. **Social Job Matching.** Social media data is already an integral part of hiring, especially for companies recruiting skilled works, the tech-savvy, and Millennial generation. Employing social media to source and screen applicants of course sends up red flags for violations of privacy, EEO, and ADA. But the genie is already out of the bottle; there's no putting her back in. While new technologies will all but guarantee discrimination and privacy challenges, laws and regulations will be revised and rewritten to meet the contemporary workplace. If not, employers will be crippled in their ability to source, recruit, and hire workers.

3. **Gamification.** Virtual reality and other forms of interactive assessment are already starting to transform the pre-hire assessment industry. Currently, they lack validation and reliability, but by blending the science of psychometrics and artificial intelligence with the art of social media, assessment tools that are engaging, relevant, and scientifically sound will emerge. Watch closely for the introduction of gamified psychometric assessments that predict job fit with better precision and meets the engagement expectations of demanding candidates.

THE GREATEST HR STORY NEVER TOLD

IN TODAY'S WORLD, knowledge is power. For the first time in history, that knowledge might be able to predict the future. It's no wonder that executives are beginning to recognize that people analytics promises to be the fuel that drives an organization's successful journey into the future.[116]

Ironically, such a discussion about the future takes us back in time, a little over a century ago, when the Industrial Revolution started to shift into high gear. A mechanical engineer named Frederick Winslow Taylor had just published a book entitled *The Principles of Scientific Management.* One of Taylor's biggest fans was automobile entrepreneur Henry Ford, founder of the Ford Motor Company.

Ford was a brilliant and successful businessman who created a demand for cars almost overnight. To keep pace with that demand, Ford had to come up with ways to manufacture more cars faster while keeping costs down. He hired Taylor, who applied his scientific management principles to the Ford production process. The rest is history.

With Taylor's help, Ford managed to reduce average production time of a Model T from more than 12 hours to 2 hours and 30 minutes.[117] Total production increased from 10,000 vehicles in one year (1908) to 10,000 vehicles in one day by 1924.[118] He lowered the cost from $850 in 1908 to under $300 in 1925.[119] Between 1913 and 1927, Ford factories produced more than 15 million Model Ts, 40% of all the cars sold in the United States.[120]

Taylor believed that making people work as hard as they could was not as efficient as optimizing the way the work was done. With a background in mechanical engineering, he applied science to any workplace task. He replaced working by "rule of thumb" with the most efficient way to perform specific tasks. Big manufacturing hitched a ride on his train and, throughout the first half of the 20th century, scientific management was applied to nearly every function of manufacturing operations. How work was performed and ways to make both workers and their work process more productive were pursued with a vengeance.[121]

Fast forward to today: Manufacturing is still a vibrant industry and Ford Motor Company is still a leading producer of automobiles. But Ford specifically, and manufacturing in general, bear little resemblance to the work, jobs, and factories of the past. The very definition of work is being redefined. How work gets done is entering unknown territory, and the role of humans in the work process is up for grabs. Surprisingly, science in management is not only back in vogue, it is an essential ingredient in 21st century productivity and performance. A century after Ford revolutionized manufacturing with principles of scientific management, it is déjà vu all over again.

But this time, it isn't science applied to just work tasks and work flow. People analytics is quite literally people-driven scientific management. It is the specialized use of the much broader analytics model called "predictive analytics" that is used to manage human resources. It looks at what makes and drives employees to be more efficient and productive. On the surface that might seem cold and exploitative. But when analytics is implemented properly with sensitivity and empathy, it also addresses the best ways to approach many growing employee concerns such as work-life balance, stress, and burnout.

Thanks to advances in technology and a precipitous drop in cost and speed, powerful predictive analytic tools are no longer exclusive to statisticians, researchers, and academics. Anyone with an interest can access the most sophisticated tools in the world, including IBM Watson, for a few dollars per day.[122] (You might be familiar with Watson from its winning performance on *Jeopardy* in 2011.[123]) Now, almost any person with a device can access one of the most powerful supercomputers in the world and find some link between people performance and background data, wage and benefits, social profiles, personality traits, work experience, education, or a multitude of other factors. In other words, IBM just democratized big data and evened the people analytics playing field between small business and the Global 500.

They aren't the only ones. New business intelligence and analytics platforms seem to pop up every day—some of them are even free and open-sourced such as R[124] and WEKA.[125] The maturity and access to people analytic tools arrived just in the nick of time, too.

Today's Measure-and-Analyze-Everything World

Every day, I receive an email notifying me how many people viewed my LinkedIn profile. I can identify each visitor and choose to connect, communicate, or ignore them. I can view in real-time how many people are visiting my website, what article or page they're reading, and how long they stay. I know which country they're from, which browser they prefer, and whether they're using a mobile device or personal computer.

I'm not unique. Nor did I purchase or develop expensive software to accomplish this. Most of the tools I use are free or cost just a few dollars each year. Analytics has been democratized; every business and consumer can track click-through rates on marketing campaigns or likes on a Facebook post. Retailers follow which products each customer views, make next purchase recommendations accordingly, and can predict with a very high probability which product(s) the customer might buy next. Healthcare providers monitor the compliance of the patient and study which combination of medications works best with the least side effects.

Despite all this measurement going on in every other business function in our organizations as well as in our personal lives, HR still lives in the dark ages of periodic reporting and time-consuming spreadsheets. Ask HR how many applicants viewed a job posting *and* started or completed an application, and you would think you had asked them to explain quantum computing. The idea of accessing such data and correlating it to the quality of hire or to attrition rates creates overwhelming angst.

Consequently, getting a timely and accurate assessment on what it takes for a company to recruit and retain employees who are both productive and engaged has been elusive. Without HR and your organization getting on board with people analytics, accessing and putting this kind of crucial information to use will only get more difficult. And HR will secure its position as senior management's assistant, devoid of any strategic relevance.

Now, I don't want to give you the wrong impression. Implementing people analytics isn't easy—it's just necessary. Software made it easier, but it isn't perfect. Whatever the circumstances, it is unequivocally more accurate than not using it at all. And, when it comes to employee screening and selection, people analytics is to HR what giving sight is to a blind person.

You need look no further than the conventional job description and interview to find out why people analytics is the solution that management needs. Remember earlier in the book when I discussed the problems with current practices of credentialing? When seeking applicants for a position, a company often sets the minimum years of experience required quite arbitrarily and artificially high in an attempt to reduce the high volume of unqualified applicants. The same holds true for the highest level of education required for candidates. Neither HR nor management can produce the evidence to back up these hunches. Undoubtedly more stringent requirements reduce the application screening workload, but they may also falsely eliminate qualified candidates.

An even better rationale to implement people analytics is the job interview. Despite hundreds of studies that question an interviewer's reliability, recruiters and managers insist their people-judging abilities and gut instinct supersede other assessment methods, including psychometric testing. What may be even more surprising is the fact that management accepts and believes this claim despite the overwhelming evidence to the contrary. The result is an interview-driven employee selection method that predicts future employee success about as well as flipping a coin does.[126]

Human bias taints our judgment no matter how good our intentions, from our subconscious reaction of an ethnic-sounding name on an application to a candidate's physical appearance. However, the right data and good analytical software can defuse this bias and predict with a higher probability the success of future hires and the retention of current employees. Evidence-based people decisions are simply better and more accurate than decisions based on the hiring manager's personal judgment or gut instinct.

In Data We Trust

This pursuit of more predictive ways to hire and manage talent isn't new. Psychologists have been studying characteristics that drive good performance since World War I. The renowned American statistician, W. Edwards Deming, once said, *"In God we trust. Everyone else, bring data."*

Two of the biggest challenges that organizations face are high turnover and attrition. It makes sense then why so many executives test the waters of people analytics with attempts to reduce turnover and attrition. It hasn't always been that way.

Let me explain. For the past few decades, HR often reached for a pre-employment test (personality, skills, or aptitude) to "fix" high turnover. They assumed that an extra screening filter might improve the quality of hire, and subsequently lower involuntary terminations. If turnover fell, the test was declared a success, even though other factors not measured by the test (e.g. a tight job market) may have played a part in the lower attrition rate. If turnover rose, managers deemed the test a failure even though factors like pay rates, benefits, supervisor ability, and even commute times might have been the cause or, at the very least, played a significant role.

With mounting pressure to acquire and retain qualified workers and skilled labor, management rightfully demands evidence that any investment in recruitment and retention is working. After years of relying on employee selection and talent management by gut instinct, executives are tired of seeing a lot of HR activity with very few tangible outcomes. They are beginning to believe that data can be extremely powerful and should be a key element in any decision, especially the decisions regarding an organization's staffing.[127]

For management to trust HR and value it as a credible partner, HR needs to rely on people analytics to provide supporting evidence and ensure its decisions align with expectations. People analytics also alters the way management thinks about HR and how HR functions.

GETTING STARTED

Human resources (HR) must embrace the fact that its sole purpose is to help the organization achieve better-than-average returns. To do this, HR needs to run itself as a business. It needs to be as effective and efficient as every other business unit such as marketing, sales, finance, and operations. It must use the best tools available, including people analytics, and stop relying on emotion, instinct and anecdotes.

What's next? You need data, and heaven knows HR certainly has plenty of it. Information overload is probably a more accurate description of all the demographic data collected from each and every employee in your organization—gender, age, ethnicity, residential location, socioeconomic status, highest level of education, years of experience, and so on. Chances are, your company just collects the data and doesn't do much more with it except use it to satisfy compliance and administrative regulations. The data may be used occasionally to prepare reports on how many paychecks were cut or how many positions remain unfilled. Beyond that, the data lies dormant or is analyzed months after an event.

It is time to change that.

As daunting as people analytics might seem, there is a silver lining. The good news is that there is a lot of room for improvement—a confession willingly made by most organizations. Research by Deloitte found that only 8% of companies believe they are optimally organized for success.[128] Only half of those companies believe they are effectively using people data to predict performance. That means there are few competitors ahead of you. Starting now gets an early jump on them and may produce an insurmountable lead. The bad news is the use of people analytics is growing exponentially. Your window of opportunity is closing as more companies are adopting people analytics every day, and catching up won't be that easy.

Data Analysis for Beginners

Before jumping into the deep end of people analytics, let's take a step back and define some common terminology.

People analytics is just a form of predictive analytics used specifically for HR. And predictive analytics is a function of data science. Since the mere mention of data science probably just caused many of you to glaze over or force you into a cold sweat, let me offer a data science for beginner's description.

You're all likely familiar with a recipe, the kind you use for baking homemade or grilling on the barbecue. Well, **data science** is simply a recipe for getting answers to questions that help predict business outcomes. Data scientists call this recipe an algorithm. The ingredients are your data. You mix the data up using a computer. And out comes your answer. Sounds pretty cool, huh?

So how is it being used? Have you ever asked "what will happen if...?" Data science helps find your answer. Companies are beginning to use data science specific for HR, to improve hiring success rates, reduce attrition, lower absenteeism and theft, identify flight risk of top performers, and build a talent pipeline of future leaders. More advanced users may even use it to predict how much employee engagement might improve if you compare an increase in the base pay rate or how pre-employment testing results correlate with increased sales.

But I'm getting a little ahead of myself. There are actually three categories of data analysis: descriptive, predictive, and prescriptive. Most companies strive to achieve at least a level of predictive analytics, but are just mired deep in "running numbers." Here is a brief description of each category.

1. **Descriptive Analytics** is the simplest and most popular form of analysis. It gives insight into easily accessed data and provides excellent insight into the past. An example might be, "How many employees left the company last month?" or "How many applicants responded to our last job posting?" The most commonly used tool to "slice and dice" descriptive data is the pivot table. Scorecards and dashboards are often used to visualize the results and help

tell a story to the rest of the company. While highly useful, descriptive analysis assumes the future will be a repeat of the past, and that is just not the case. In spite of its limitations, mastering descriptive analytics is a rite of passage to more advanced analytics.

2. **Predictive analytics** is a more advanced category of data analysis and more forward-looking than the analysis the majority of organizations currently use. It is more sophisticated data mining than the slice and dice of descriptive analysis because it includes forecasting. Predictive analytics answers the questions, "What will happen?" and, "Why will it happen?" It asks questions such as "How many people are expected to leave in the next month?" and, "How will increased investment in Learning & Development impact next year's performance?" More advanced predictive analysis employs regression analysis or advanced machine learning like decision trees and neural networks to find answers. Predictive analytics typically requires advanced to expert knowledge in statistics and data analysis. Many organizations either hire a data scientist or partner with outside consultants.

3. **Prescriptive analytics** is the Holy Grail of people analytics. It provides answers to two very important questions. "What should we do?" and, "Why should we do it?" It doesn't just influence decisions toward the highest probability of success, but it also gives advice and helps managers take appropriate action. Instead of posting a job and waiting for a response, prescriptive analytics recommends the best place to post your listing, predicts how many applicants might

apply, and provides an accurate estimate of the time it will take to fill the position. Prescriptive analytics transforms exercises like scenario planning and brainstorming into optimized decision-making.

GROWING UP IS SOMETIMES HARD TO DO

Remember my story earlier about asking Alexa or Siri for its recommendation on hiring? Because advanced technology will be available doesn't mean you get to pick the next generation device off the shelf and it comes loaded with your choice of descriptive, predictive, and prescriptive analytics. These types of outcomes don't occur on-demand. An organization needs clean, structured data—and lots of it. Predictive and prescriptive outcomes take time, resources, and money.

That's why there is no time like the present to begin. Regardless of whatever additional advancements in technology time will bring, there is no such thing as "leapfrogging" when it comes to data analysis. Organizations must start with descriptive analysis, grow into high probability decisions with predictive analytics, and then eventually develop the ability to prescribe outcomes.

To get started on the people analytics journey, Josh Bersin and his team at Deloitte made it easy to assess how "mature" an organization is when it comes to people analytics. They developed the Talent Analytics Maturity Model[129] which provides your company with a convenient guide to help identify where you need to start or how far you've traveled on this journey. They use slightly different categories of analysis than I do but the pathway is the same. The three categories I described earlier are noted in the parentheses.

Level 4: Predictive Analytics (Prescriptive)

Level 3: Advanced Analytics (Predictive)

Level 2: Advanced Reporting (Descriptive)

Level 1: Operational Reporting (Descriptive)

Most companies (86%), according to Deloitte, are currently stuck at Level 1 or 2. Level 1 organizations focus on operational reporting using data. They track headcount, cost of labor, and number of employees who left the company or didn't show up on any given day. It's historical data used mostly for compliance and to critique past events. Level 2 companies rely more on metrics and might utilize dashboards and benchmarking to compare results to other organizations, industries, or best practice standards. A Level 2 metric might be the cost per hire, time to fill, or candidate abandonment rates.

Keeping the reporting up-to-date is time consuming for Level 1, and the information is typically weeks, if not months old. Data is likely scattered within different departments and protected by technical and political firewalls. The reports generated at Level 1 are used typically to justify activity and comply with budget requirements. Day-to-day decisions are still guided by opinion, assumption, and intuition. Evidence-based and predictive decision-making is only a topic at the annual budget meeting. As a result, HR lacks credibility and is excluded from management's strategic discussions. Without analytics, Level 1 organizations are constantly trying to drive forward by using the rearview mirror.

Many level 2 companies use a Human Resource Information System (HRIS) or Applicant Processing Software (APS) to track and keep employee records. Reporting is more efficient, and the data can be timelier. However, Level 2 is still stuck in reporting mode, which relegates HR to being simply an administrative assistant to management. Executives and managers take the information, and may or may not use it. Without advanced analytics to support HR's talent acquisition and retention recommendations and decisions, it isn't uncommon for executives to question the validity of the information when it doesn't support their agenda.

Once HR makes the leap from reporting to analytics, it's a whole new ball game. Level 3 HR earns a seat at the table by relying on the numbers to do the talking. Management now sees HR as having the ability to increase value to the business and the bottom line. Other executives look to them to help predict the impact of policy changes. HR assumes the role of a data squad, and applies statistical modeling to solve each business problem. HR departments that achieve Level 3 status transition from tracking turnover to assessing the flight-risk of top talent in critical roles.

Only 4% of organizations (as of 2016) have reached Level 4. At this level, it's possible to forecast with high probability what will happen in the future—how many employees might be needed and where leadership gaps will exist. HR at Level 4 is called upon to participate and even lead scenario and workforce planning. Level 4 people analytics is where the data guides the talent and the talent drives outcomes. But, like so many other strategies, Level 4 won't be achieved by purchasing the best software and appointing a team. Level 4 companies experience a culture shift where data and talent live in harmony, and evidence is the universal language shared from top to bottom.

What Can Go Wrong?

It's no longer a choice *if* you must use predictive analytics but *when* you need to get started and *how fast* you must get up to speed. The allure of even small improvements means more productivity, better performance, and lower cost. The promise and benefits of big data indicate that, like it or not, everyone will need to get better at predicting the future.

While we can likely all agree HR can put their hands on a lot of data, they will need access to data from a variety of sources, and that may prove challenging. In fact, getting your hands on good clean, structured data is often the single biggest barrier an organization faces. HR will likely confront a few departmental silos too. Some departments might be territorial and be concerned with what problems might be uncovered. Others likely have concerns about privacy and confidentiality.

Even when all the parties agree to cooperate, the data from other sources might not be compatible or complete. Unless the organization utilizes an enterprise software practice that includes every business function, data might be collected and stored in different software or different formats. Cleaning it and making it compatible will take time and resources. People analytics has a long learning curve and longer ramp-up time. There's no such thing as a rapid start. But whatever the challenges, the rewards of evidence-based decision making, better hiring decisions, less attrition, and higher engagement will be worth it.

But let's not fool ourselves. Accumulating lots of data and analyzing it isn't bullet-proof. Any predictive model still relies on assumptions despite them becoming less trustworthy with each passing day. On top of that, today's business environment is more volatile, uncertain, complex, and ambiguous (VUCA) than ever. Today's VUCA environment makes it even more important to find ways to differentiate assumptions from fact and to monitor things closely.

What are some other reasons why people analytics can go wrong?

Don't confuse causational with correlational.[130] According to the Bureau of Statistics, correlation is, *"A statistical measure (expressed as a number) that describes the size and direction of a relationship between two or more variables."* [Causation] *"indicates that one event is the result of the occurrence of the other event; i.e. there is a causal relationship between the two events. This is also referred to as cause and effect."*

Here is a classic example. A study of turnover by manager indicates one particular department experienced an extraordinary amount of turnover. Did the manager cause it or was there just a coincidental relationship?

As a rule of thumb, trust correlations but avoid making easy conclusions about causation. There are often other subtle variables that play a role in explaining each correlation, and these variations may not be included in your data. In the case of the manager, other causes might be shift-work, location, demographics, competition for skilled labor, or pay. A common outcome of deep analytics is the revelation of the cause—or that you might need more or different data.

Let's take another example of correlation and causation from my world of employee testing. Conscientiousness is a trait included in many pre-employment tests; studies indicate high conscientiousness provides reliable insight into lower absenteeism rates and overall dependability. Conscientiousness may correlate well with absenteeism, but it doesn't prevent or cause it. A lot of variables exist that may impact or influence attendance, including commute time, transportation, caregiving responsibility, personal motivation, and job engagement, to name just a few.

Context is also important when assessing and comparing employees. Joe is ready to hire Sue who recently moved to the area. Every reference gave rave reviews, and all agreed they would hire Sue back in a heartbeat. But your company is smaller, and Sue's responsibilities are much greater than what she's experienced before. How much of Sue's past performance that contributed to her success has been due to her own doing versus support by a great team? Was Sue's success a product of her ability or the environment?

What about the top performing salesperson who is recruited away from a competitor and then flops at your company? While he touts a long list of achievements, how much did the company contribute to his success with a strong training program, managers who mentored and coached, and a fabulous lead generation program? Unless you put the analysis in context, your results may miss expectations.

And the last, but surely not least, reason—**the self-fulfilling prophecy.** Outcomes can be influenced by one's expectations—that's just human nature. Until advanced machine-learning and artificial intelligence supplants human input, there is still a risk for tainted data. When we expect a certain outcome, we are more likely to look for and include evidence that confirms our hypotheses and ignore or exclude evidence to the contrary. Pay attention and always ask, "Did I really find a correlation (or a cause) or did I just find what I was looking for?" Or another way to ask it, "What am I denying that the data is telling me?"

It is worth noting that data analytics shouldn't be seen as a means to a predictive end but as a means to asking better questions and carrying out better discovery. All research begins with one or more "what if" questions.

» What if we use another recruiting source?

» What if we increase wages or offer a bonus?

» What if we change the minimum years of experience required?

Those questions inevitably lead to "I wonder" inquiries.

» I wonder how turnover is affected by the supervisor or commute time?

» I wonder if the pre-employment test is helping minimize absenteeism or predict flight risk?

And then you have the convergence factor that asks:

» I wonder if there are correlations between, base pay increases, health care benefits, talent acquisition, and employee satisfaction?

The executives at Wegmans Food Markets wondered which benefits its employees valued the most. Rather than arbitrarily changing its employee benefits package to reduce costs, they first asked if a 5% base pay increase combined with a lower health insurance deductible would maintain or reduce employee satisfaction compared to a simple 10% pay increase.[131]

Wegmans found that health benefits were a critical driver for employees to join and stay at the organization even for employees who were not currently eligible. The result of the analysis was $107 investment per non-eligible employee would cost $1.5 million but would feel like $32.5 million to the employees. Accordingly, Wegmans was able to control costs without reducing employee satisfaction. Incidentally, base pay was ranked at the bottom of the list for perceived employee value

It is nothing short of amazing how clear the future becomes during the preparation and manipulation of data within the context of people analytics. The metric you sought to measure often prompts questions about whether you need an alternate metric, which leads to changes that result in more meaningfully measurable improvement. The end game seems to be the pursuit of metrics that "move the needle." Without analytics, finding that needle may feel like a game of Whack-a-Mole. That's no way to run a business.

Predictive analytics is also alluring, because it allows us to expand the range of relationships beyond what conventional methods permit. With advanced technology, the dots can be connected between pieces of information that were never considered to be connected before. Conventional reporting just doesn't capture anything close to what statistical and analytics software can. People analytics gives us the ability to see new correlations and patterns across seemingly unrelated assumptions, databases and systems because in a complex system, elements can potentially interact in different ways each time because they are interdependent.

In turn, recognizing and leveraging this fluidity gives companies a distinctive vantage point in making better recruitment, hiring, and retention decisions. HR transforms from a retrospective and reactive administrative function to a strategic partner whose predictive models predict employee behaviors, attitudes, and capabilities that drive business outcomes.

People Analytics Can Be Weird Too

At what point does predictive analytics become creepy? A *Wall Street Journal* article reported on Google's algorithm that determines which employees are most likely to quit.[132]This helped Google *"get inside people's heads before they know they might leave,"* shared former Senior Vice President of People Operations, Lazlo Bock. Will the employee be blown away when the manager approaches them with a new career role or freaked out by what he perceives as eavesdropping or mind reading by Big Brother?

And then, there is the question of fairness. There are some things employees can't control, like IQ, personality, and family background. What if the data discovers a correlation between an IQ of 100, being raised by a single parent, and extroversion with the likelihood of working hard or with the likelihood of employee theft? Is it fair to use factors a candidate or employee can't control? That suggests the story of a future like the one described in the movie *Minority Report*, in which law enforcement could tell who would commit a crime in the future, so the police arrested those people in advance.

In the future, simply having access to the data for predictive modeling won't be enough. Smart competitors will use analytics to make real-time decisions that are prescriptive, automated, and scalable. This is the very same evolution that occurred during the Industrial Revolution when mass production replaced the artisan who manufactured one product at a time. Algorithms are already being used by banks to detect potential fraud, and by airlines to re-route passengers in bad weather. Why not use the data to predict when to hire, who to hire, and how to form the most productive teams?

The most successful recipe for the use of big data in people analytics will embrace the rigor of analysis, a dose of humanity, and a dash of practicality. It also requires a new set of management, operational, and financial disciplines. How we balance fairness and unintended consequences with an employer's interest in hiring and retaining better employees is a difficult question to answer but one that needs immediate and ongoing attention. Reading the data that lies at our fingertips forces us to ask difficult questions like, "What hiring assumptions are we making that may run counter to the evidence?" or "Why do some candidates perform better than others?" and "Why do some teams get better outcomes?" How organizations implement these changes still requires a human element.

High performing organizations will leverage the power of analytics by channeling their efforts within this new evidence based paradigm. This promotes agility, fast execution, and precision. If your organization hasn't yet joined the people analytics revolution, it is time that it did.

Making predictive analytics operational is not optional. Start by asking these three questions:

» At what level of people analytics maturity is our organization?

» How committed is our management to evidence-based decision-making?

» Who will own people analytics in our organization? (HR may be the rightful heir to leading and managing this transformation, but that might not be enough. The inconvenient truth is management's uncertainty if HR leaders are prepared and if so, is management willing to sponsor HR?)

Make sure you check out the people analytics effectiveness and readiness worksheets I included in the Addendum to help you jumpstart a discussion and get started on the journey.

KEY POINTS

» The sole purpose of HR is to help its organization achieve better than average returns on investment.

» Companies are beginning to use data science specific for HR called people analytics to improve hiring success rates, reduce attrition, identify flight risk, build a leadership pipeline, and correlate pay and rewards with performance.

» For management to trust HR and value it as a credible strategic partner, HR needs to provide supporting evidence for its decisions.

» People analytics isn't easy or perfect but it is absolutely essential.

QUESTIONS

» People analytics helps companies make better decisions about:

» Sourcing – What are our best sources for each position?

» Recruiting – How do we compete for top talent?

» Selection – Who should we hire?

» On-boarding – How quickly are new hires productive?

» Retention – How do we get top talent to stay?

» Performance management – How do we make our people better?

» Training and development – What skills need to be developed first?

» Succession planning – Who should lead and when?

» Compensation and benefits – How should we pay and reward?

Favorite Quotes about Analytics

In God we trust, all others must bring data.

W. Edwards Deming

What gets measured gets managed.

Peter Drucker

The price of light is less than the cost of darkness.

Arthur C. Nielsen

Without big data analytics, companies are blind and deaf, wandering out onto the Web like deer on a freeway.

Geoffrey Moore

A point of view can be a dangerous luxury when substituted for insight and understanding.

Marshall McLuhan

He uses statistics as a drunken man uses lamp posts—for support rather than for illumination."

Andrew Lang

Not everything that can be counted counts, and not everything that counts can be counted.

Albert Einstein

If you don't know how to ask the right questions, you discover nothing.

W. Edward Deming

Statistics are like bikinis. What they reveal is suggestive, but what they conceal is vital.

Aaron Levenstein

If you torture the data long enough, it will confess.

Ronald Coase

The alchemists in their search for gold discovered many other things of greater value.

Arthur Schopenhauer

Once we know something, we find it hard to imagine what it was like not to know it.

Chip & Dan Heath

If you can't explain it simply, you don't understand it well enough.

Albert Einstein

If the statistics are boring, you've got the wrong numbers.

Edward Tufte

The greatest value of a picture is when it forces us to notice what we never expected to see.

John Tukey

TOMORROW

What's Next?

D EFINITELY MAYBE IS AS ACCURATE AS IT GETS WHEN TRYING TO PREDICT THE FUTURE. NO ONE HAS FOUND THE CRYSTAL BALL—AT LEAST NOT YET. THERE ARE A FEW TRENDS HOWEVER THAT ARE REALLY GOOD BETS TO CONTINUE.

1. Tomorrow will be exponentially different from today.

2. VUCA will continue to be a brilliant and accurate description of the environment in which we work, live, and play.

3. Recruiting top talent will grow increasingly more challenging. Retaining the talent will be even harder.

4. Organizations will aggressively implement people analytics and religiously rely on it to guide every human resources decision.

I started out this book by saying "it has been by far the most difficult to write." It never got easier. At one point, my wife burst into my office and turned on the news. The lead story was about a self-driving, robotic truck. The prediction was that *sometime toward the end of the year (2017), we could be doing this [delivery] without a person behind the wheel.*"[133]

It wasn't the first self-driving truck that made such a headline. In the fall of 2016, a truck owned by Otto made headlines by driving itself across Colorado to deliver a shipment of beer. What was once considered a sci-fi fantasy is now a universal prediction: autonomous trucks will be commonplace on our highways by 2022 at the latest. That puts nearly 3.5 million U.S. truck driver jobs in jeopardy without mentioning the 180,000 taxi drivers and 600,000 Uber drivers when the autonomous automobile hits the road.

Then in the final minutes before sending my manuscript to my publisher for layout, a text message alerted me to Volvo's decision to stop designing combustion-engine only cars by 2019. More news came that Norway wants to ban fuel-burning cars by 2025; France proposed to outlaw all petrol and diesel vehicles by 2040; and all new cars sold in Europe could be electric by 2035.

The question about what's next must extend to 2nd and 3rd level consequences of these changes. When talking about autonomous vehicles, what happens to the clerks who work at the convenience stores and truck stops when fewer customers stop and shop? Who's to say that the passengers in these autonomous vehicles won't order from Amazon which delivers their snacks and coffees by drone? What happens to the tax revenues collected from the consumption of gasoline when an electric battery replaces the gas tank?

Autonomous vehicles are just the tip of the iceberg of what life will be after the next round of exponential change. In the same CBS story about Otto, they shared how Amazon is opening its first cashier-less automated grocery store. A system of sensors and cameras observe what you've taken off the shelf and charges you automatically without ever encountering an employee. "You're going to end up with the equivalent of Walmart with a handful of employees," Martin Ford, author of the book *Rise of the Robots* said. The story didn't end there. It reported on the pizza shop that uses four specialized robots to help make the pizza. The company plans to replace the remaining humans on the line, too.

What started out not too long ago as a trickle of stories on exponential change is now a flood. My inbox is always full. In the past week, I read stories about:

» The first heart cell[134] and titanium bone parts[135] have been 3D printed.

» A patient-specific 3D liver[136] was printed for less than $150.[137]

» Artificial intelligence that can read lips is now available.[138]

» A full-size house was 3D-printed in 24 hours.[139]

» A scientist is 3D-printing blood vessels for sick children.[140]

» Artificial intelligence will allow each person to be the "CEO" of his/her own health.[141]

» Sensors are quickly allowing the diagnosis and treatment of many diseases on a smartphone app.[142]

» Adidas announced plans to mass-produce 3D printed shoes.[143]

» Virtual Reality in grocery stores—instead of shopping for products on a website, immerse yourself in a virtual store and "stroll" up and down the aisles the same way you do in a brick-and-mortar store.[144]

» JPMorgan Chase & Co now uses software to interpret commercial loans, reducing 360,000 hours of lawyer time each year.[145]

» AI software that identifies leukemia in photos and X-rays, learning faster than technicians.[146]

» Amazon.com reduced new hire training to two days because of its newest robotics used in shipping.[147]

» Insurance companies introduced software that can view a picture of your dented car, identify the make and model of the car, and compute the amount of the claim.[148]

» Software can read X-rays almost twice as well as seasoned radiologists.[149]

» Voice recognition can type 300% faster than a human.[150]

No matter how excited or scared we feel about the future, we can't just ignore the occasional weirdness that comes with it. Among the headlines that caught my attention recently was this: *A Man Married a Robot He Built Himself.* Yes, you read that correctly. A Chinese engineer facing the realities of a widening gender gap in China built himself a robot bride.[151]

Beyond different and weird, change opens up a deluge of ethical, moral, and privacy questions. I deliberately didn't address them in this book. For now, I'm leaving that up to business and community leaders as well as our elected officials. New norms must be decided in the communities and countries in which we live.

We're crossing into uncharted territory with the convergence of gene editing, robotics, sensors, 3D printing, and artificial intelligence. What constitutes life and death and everything in between seems open to debate. The blurring of lines between privacy and security is already mainstream conversation.

My sole purpose in writing this book was to introduce how exponential change will disrupt the world we knew, how it will change the world of work and jobs, and how companies and individuals will need to adapt. If I left you asking more questions about the future than giving you answers, then I have succeeded.

Regardless of our age, gender, race, or ethnicity, we are all on a journey that is only 1% complete. Take your first step by asking yourself what has become my favorite question:

What technological disruption could bankrupt my business or end my career in the next 2 to 3 years?

And specific to *Recruiting in the Age of Googlization*:

What technological disruption or event could interfere with our ability to recruit, hire, and retain top talent in the next 2 to 3 years?

There is no right or wrong answer to these questions with these two exceptions: "Nothing" and "I don't know" are both unacceptable answers!

A Final Word

TECHNOLOGICAL ADVANCEMENT is accelerating at an exponential pace. Predictions of artificial intelligence, machine learning, and other disruptive technologies like 3D-printing and robotics are no longer science fiction, but reality. As a result, a massive shift is underway in the way work gets done, jobs get defined, the workplace is designed, and people are managed. The recruitment and retention of top talent seems like a perpetually moving target.

Regardless how exhaustive and focused the effort to regain control, it never seems to be enough. Nearly everyone underestimates the accelerating rate and scope of exponential change. That's why *Recruiting in the Age of Googlization* has become and will remain one of the top challenges keeping CEOs awake at night.

But all is not lost. Despite the unprecedented difficulty in attracting (and retaining) top talent, quite a few organizations have found ways to overcome such a formidable adversary and attain the upper hand. Let me share a few of their secrets.

1. Act as if you have a bullseye on your back...because you do. The future isn't coming. It's here. It's no longer a matter of *if* you will be affected, but *when* and by *how much*.

When competitors aren't targeting your best employees, exponential change is lurking right behind to disrupt and maybe even destroy your business model. You can't act too aggressively when it comes to recruitment and retention of top talent these days.

2. Identify and quarantine enemies of change within your organization. The urge to resist change is compelling especially when industry leaders attempt to allay fears. Don't believe me? Look no further than the demise of once powerful retailers like Sears, JC Penney, and Blockbuster, Internet legends AOL and Yahoo, or the iconic Eastman Kodak. Lack of urgency and hubris are company killers when it comes to exponential change.

3. Identify and embrace champions of change. Not every idea is a winner. But creativity and innovation are critical components of contemporary company culture. This is the perfect opportunity to engage the maligned Millennials and Gen Z. Instead of pointing fingers at them; engage them. Ask "what and how might new technologies disrupt my products, services, and business model within the next 24 months?"

4. Info-sponge. The lethal blow to your bestselling product or time-tested business model is not likely to come from a known competitor. There is a business like Netflix, Uber, Airbnb, Amazon, or Apple just waiting to burst onto the scene. Each of these businesses disrupted industries once deemed untouchable. They embraced and cross-pollinated ideas with no regard to the conventions and norms of past success. Follow the lead of Priceline co-founder Jeff

Hoffman who takes a few minutes each morning to read an article or listen to a podcast from a completely unrelated business or industry and ask "how can this be applied to my business?"

ACKNOWLEDGMENTS

COMPLETING THIS BOOK took more than just one man's effort. It took a village.

I couldn't have done it without the unwavering support, enthusiasm, and love from my wife, Jerry. Whenever I got lost, distracted, *and* frustrated, she always encouraged me to keep going. I couldn't possibly have completed this book without her.

Special thanks to my mother too who believes you are never too old to learn. She is an amazing mother and friend and will always be an inspiration and role model for living life to the fullest.

To the two very best strategic business partners and dear friends, Judy Suiter and Michael Spremulli, one could ever ask for. Together we have redefined collaboration and camaraderie for nearly two decades and have affirmed how "co-opetition" is supposed to work.

To my colleague, friend, and mentor John Dame for his wisdom, support, and guidance.

To the many-dedicated-consultants-and-colleagues-I'd-like-to-mention-but-unfortunately-don't-have-room-to-list who have shared their professional journey with me through many conversations, emails, phone calls, interviews, and podcasts.

To Steve Schulz for allowing me to put my thoughts on paper and for sharing them in his *Business2Business Magazines* for over 16 years.

To the dozens of editors, bloggers, podcasters, and writers who have solicited my opinions and have shared my advice and recommendations with thousands of organizations and people.

To the TEDx Lehigh River committee, speakers, and team of coaches who stuck with me and helped me give voice to an idea worth spreading.

To my friends, colleagues, and clients who value our relationships, celebrate success with me, and challenge me to grow. Thank you for sharing with me your collective wisdom, ambition, and tolerance.

I encourage you too to share your thoughts, comments, recommendations, personal stories, and experiences with me. How is exponential change influencing and impacting your business and personal life? How are you dealing with VUCA—volatility, uncertainty, complexity, and ambiguity? What's working and what's not?

Call me. Send emails to shift@super-solutions.com. Connect with me on LinkedIn, Twitter, and Facebook.

Ira S Wolfe

About the Author

ENTREPRENEUR, AUTHOR AND TEDx Speaker Ira S. Wolfe took the most unlikely of career pathways to becoming one of the most prominent and influential thought leaders in human resources today. Before starting Success Performance Solutions over two decades ago, Wolfe was a dentist who "loved everything about dentistry but dentistry." After 18 very successful years, he walked away. Instead of filling holes in teeth, he began to help businesses fill job and leadership vacancies. Armed with an uncanny ability to assess employee job fit, build high performing teams, and foresee disruptive workforce trends, Wolfe became the employee selection lynchpin for many organizations. His first book *The Perfect Labor Storm* launched him onto the national stage which was followed by *Geeks, Geezers, and Googlization*. His 2016 TEDx Talk, *Make Change Work for You,* became the inspiration for his latest book *Recruiting in the Age of Googlization: When the Shift Hits Your Plan.*

When he's not working with clients, Wolfe is a prolific business writer, blogger, and podcaster. He is a contributing writer for Forbes, CornerstoneOnDemand's ReWork, Huffington Post, Lehigh Valley Business Journal, Business2BusinessMagazine, and several regional and industry business journals. He's been featured in INC Magazine, Fast Company, American Express OPEN

Forum, Business Week, NFIB, Inc., Intuit Small Business and Fox Business.

Wolfe lives in the Lehigh Valley (PA) near the foothills of the Pocono Mountains with his high school sweetheart.

ADDENDUM

RECRUITING PROCESS AUDIT WORKSHEET

1. Which sources are you using to recruit candidates?

2. How much are investing each month in each source?

3. How are you receiving and compiling the applications and resumes from each source?

4. How are you filtering and screening applications from each source?

5. What type of reports can you generate from each source?

6. Are you currently using staffing agencies or outside recruiters to fill open positions?

7. If yes, what percentage of your open positions are filled using these recruiting agencies?

8. Which social media platforms are you using to promote open jobs?

9. Do you offer job seekers or candidates the ability to contact you with questions in real-time? (Chat, text, phone, social media)

10. If using an applicant tracking system, must all candidates apply through the system? If no, how are those applications reviewed and tracked?

11. What happens after a candidate applies?

    a. Do they receive an email?

    b. How quickly do you contact them?

    c. How many days or weeks does it take you to hire from application to job offer?

    d. When and how do you communicate with unqualified applicants?

RECRUITING EFFECTIVENESS AUDIT WORKSHEET

1. How many views do you get for each job posting by source (including social media)?

2. What percentage of views come from desktop vs tablet vs smartphone users?

3. How many job seekers click to apply?

4. What percentage of job seekers start an application (by job and source)?

5. How many candidates complete an application (by job and source)?

6. What are your most effective sources by positions?

7. What is your cost-to-obtain a completed application by source?

8. What is your cost-to hire per position?

9. What is your cost-to-hire by source?

10. What is your time-to-hire per position (job requisition to job filled)?

11. Are you measuring the quality of hire and if so, how?

12. Are you measuring time-to-fill, turnover, and quality of hire by source, department, and/or manager?

Do We Really Need People Analytics in Our Organization?

1. Do we have the evidence to support the people management assumptions and decisions we make about:
   a. Talent acquisition?
   b. Employee selection and promotion?
   c. Attrition and employee turnover?
   d. Absenteeism and employee theft?
   e. Compensation, benefits, and rewards?
   f. Return on investment for training?
   g. Leadership pipeline?
   h. Proposed policy changes?

2. Do we have data available right now to back up HR decisions we made in the past:

   24 hours   7 days   30 days   90 days

3. Do we have data available right now to make a good decision on HR events that will occur in the next:

   24 hours   7 days   30 days   90 days

If you answered NO to any of these questions, the answer is a resounding YES.

QUESTIONS TO ASK BEFORE GETTING STARTED WITH PEOPLE ANALYTICS?

1. What problem are we trying to solve?

2. What data do we need?

3. What sources of data do we have that we should be using but don't?

4. Where is the data stored?

5. Is all the data integrated (vs stored on multiple platforms, systems or departments)?

6. What form is it in (digitized vs paper)?

7. Who do we need to contact to access the data?

8. How would we access the data?

9. Is the data structured or unstructured?

10. Is the data accurate?

11. Is the data clean?

12. What privacy or confidentiality hurdles might we face?

13. What safeguards should be constructed to avoid invasion of employee privacy?

14. Once we have the data, who has the skills to run the analytics?

15. What others factors are we not considering now but should?

HR PEOPLE ANALYTICS READINESS AUDIT

Strongly Agree – 6   Mostly Agree – 5
Slightly Agree – 4   Slightly Disagree – 3
Mostly Disagree – 2   Completely Disagree – 1

1. Management in our organization has embraced people analytics as an essential driver of business outcomes.	
2. Management has identified an executive sponsor to spearhead people analytics in our organization.	
3. HR provides management with data-driven evidence to back up its recruitment decisions.	
4. HR provides management with data-driven evidence to back up its retention decisions.	
5. HR provides management with data-driven evidence to back up its performance management decisions.	
6. HR provides management with data driven evidence to back up its recommendations for compensation, rewards, and training.	
7. HR provides management with dashboards using relevant and current metrics to adjust recruitment and retention strategies on the fly.	
8. HR provides management with attrition rates for different groups of employees such as high vs low potentials.	
9. HR provides management with "flight risk" rates to know when top talent in critical roles might leave.	
10. Our current HR team has the skills and knowledge to implement and integrate people analytics into its decision-making process.	
Total	

50 – 60 points: Congratulations, you're a people data scientist!

40 – 49 points: You're well on your way to securing a seat at the executive table.

30 – 39 points: Ho-hum, you need to show more proof!

0 – 29 points: You seem to be stuck in HR's weeds.

MORE BOOKS BY IRA S WOLFE

Perfect Labor Storm Fact Book

Perfect Labor Storm 2.0

Understanding Business Values and Motivators

Geeks, Geezers, and Googlization

Notes

1. https://electrek.co/2017/06/21/all-electric-aircraft-eviation/

2. http://www.theverge.com/2017/4/24/15406208/larry-page-flying-car-kitty-hawk-flyer-prototype

3. http://www.visualcapitalist.com/extraordinary-size-amazon-one-chart/

4. http://www.oxfordmartin.ox.ac.uk/downloads/academic/The_Future_of_Employment.pdf

5. https://www.technologyreview.com/s/603431/as-goldman-embraces-automation-even-the-masters-of-the-universe-are-threatened/

6. http://www.zerohedge.com/news/2017-03-28/robots-win-blackrock-bets-computers-over-human-stock-pickers-fires-dozens

7. http://www.reuters.com/article/us-bank-of-america-idUSKBN15M2DY

8. https://www.technologyreview.com/s/602896/fedex-bets-on-automation-as-it-prepares-to-fend-off-uber-and-amazon/

9. http://www.wsj.com/livecoverage/berkshire-hathaway-2017-annual-meeting-analysis/card/1494084399

10. https://www.wired.com/insights/2014/11/the-internet-of-things-bigger/

11. http://www.oxfordmartin.ox.ac.uk/downloads/academic/
    The_Future_of_Employment.pdf
12. https://hbr.org/2014/01/what-vuca-really-means-for-you
13. http://www2.deloitte.com/us/en/pages/risk/articles/de-
    loitte-on-disruption.html
14. http://bit.ly/futureshockquote
15. http://www.audiotech.com/trends-magazine/fourth-indus-
    trial-revolution-gains-momentum/
16. https://www.wired.com/2006/04/war/
17. https://www.atkearney.com/strategy/ideas-insights/arti-
    cle/-/asset_publisher/LCcgOeS4t85g/content/winning-in-
    a-turbulent-world/10192
18. http://www.mckinsey.com/business-functions/strate-
    gy-and-corporate-finance/our-insights/the-four-global-
    forces-breaking-all-the-trends
19. http://www.business2businessonline.com/pdfContent/
    VUCA-Ready%20Management.pdf
20. https://www.nytimes.com/2015/07/23/arts/international/
    photos-photos-everywhere.html
21. https://youtu.be/Mx8qYmkV5NQ
22. https://www.theatlantic.com/business/archive/2015/04/
    where-do-firms-go-when-they-die/390249/
23. Babson Olin School of business, Fast Company April
    2011, page 121
24. https://www.foreignaffairs.com/articles/2016-06-13/hu-
    man-work-robotic-future
25. http://www.businessinsider.com/mcdonalds-ex-ceo-takes-
    on-minimum-wage-2016-5
26. http://www.oxfordmartin.ox.ac.uk/downloads/academic/
    The_Future_of_Employment.pdf

27. https://www.weforum.org/agenda/2015/08/how-technology-will-change-the-way-we-work/

28. http://www.fastcompany.com/3061396/the-future-of-work/why-even-the-c-suite-might-not-be-safe-from-automation

29. https://www.wired.com/2017/03/baxter-robot-fixes-mistakes-reading-mind/

30. https://www.caseyresearch.com/articles/brain-vs-computer

31. http://vucabook.com/the-pace-of-change-in-the-vuca-world/

32. http://www.sciencealert.com/google-s-quantum-computer-is-100-million-times-faster-than-your-laptop

33. http://www.allstateinvestors.com/phoenix.zhtml

34. http://www3.weforum.org/docs/WEF_GAC15_Technological_Tipping_Points_report_2015.pdf

35. Ibid.

36. http://www.oxfordmartin.ox.ac.uk/downloads/academic/The_Future_of_Employment.pdf

37. Ibid.

38. http://www.pwc.co.uk/services/human-resource-services/human-resource-consulting/organisations-dont-have-the-right-skills-to-lead-transformational-change.html

39. http://execdev.kenan-flagler.unc.edu/blog/leadership-development-in-a-vuca-environment

40. Lawrence Kirk, Leadership in a VUCA World (UNC Kenan-Flagler Business School, 2013)

41. http://vucabook.com/the-pace-of-change-in-the-vuca-world/

42. http://www.wisdomatwork.com/wp-content/uploads/VUCA-Savvy-Leader-MWorld-Sum-2013-Levey.pdf

43. http://www.growbold.com/2013/developing-leaders-in-a-vuca-environment_UNC.2013.pdf

44. https://www.forbes.com/sites/joshbersin/2016/03/03/why-a-focus-on-teams-not-just-leaders-is-the-secret-to-business-performance/#2b91162024d5

45. http://mindsetonline.com/

46. Bill Weller and Jean Egmon. "The Prepared Mind of a Leader: Eight Skills Leaders Use to Innovate, Make Decisions, and Solve Problems: Amazon.com: Books. Jossey-Bass, n.d. Web. 01 Apr 2017

47. Ibid.

48. Gordon, Edward E. Winning the global talent showdown: how businesses and communities can partner to rebuild the jobs pipeline. San Francisco: Berrett-Koehler Publishers, 2009, p 2.

49. https://www.bls.gov/mlr/1999/12/art1full.pdf

50. http://www.oxfordmartin.ox.ac.uk/downloads/academic/The_Future_of_Employment.pdf

51. http://marcprensky.com/digital-native/

52. Friedman, Thomas L., Thank You for Being Late: An Optimist's Guide to Thriving in the Age of Accelerations (Kindle Locations 3499-3503). Farrar, Straus, and Giroux, Kindle Edition.

53. Ibid, Kindle Locations 3622-3663.

54. https://reports.weforum.org/future-of-jobs-2016/chapter-1-the-future-of-jobs-and-skills/

55. https://www.bls.gov/ooh/installation-maintenance-and-repair/heating-air-conditioning-and-refrigeration-mechanics-and-installers.htm#tab-6

56. http://www.emergingobjects.com/2015/03/07/cool-brick/

57.   http://www.businessinsider.com/robots-will-steal-your-
      job-citi-ai-increase-unemployment-inequality-2016-2

58.   https://www.shrm.org/hr-today/news/hr-news/pages/inno-
      vation-curiosity-collaboration-nonroutine.aspx

59.   http://www.perfectlaborstorm.com/2012/04/whos-to-
      blame-for-job-skill-shortages-employers-workers-or-schools/

60.   http://www.businessinsider.com/robots-will-steal-your-
      job-citi-ai-increase-unemployment-inequality-2016-2

61.   Friedman, Thomas L., Thank You for Being Late, Kindle
      Locations 3796-3798

62.   http://member.iftf.org/futureofwork

63.   http://edglossary.org/growth-mindset/

64.   Friedman, Thomas L., Thank You for Being Late, Kindle
      Locations 3456-3547

65.   https://hbr.org/2014/08/curiosity-is-as-important-as-intel-
      ligence

66.   http://www.businessinsider.com/conscientiousness-pre-
      dicts-success-2014-4

67.   http://www.rethinkrobotics.com/build-a-bot/

68.   http://www.rossintelligence.com/

69.   PayScale. (2016). 2016 Workforce-Skills Preparedness Re-
      port. Retrieved from http://www.payscale.com/data-pack-
      ages/job-skills

70.   http://www.burrus.com/2016/04/can-disruptive-ask-
      ing-simple-question/

71.   Blivin, Jamai, and Ben Wallerstein. "SHIFT HAPPENS
      - static1.squarespace.com." Shift Happens. Innovate Edu-
      cate, n.d. Web. 29 Mar. 2017

72.   Georgetown Center on Education and the Workforce.
      (2013). Recovery: Job Growth and Education Requirements

Through 2020. Retrieved from https://cew.georgetown.edu/ wp-content/ uploads/2014/11/Recovery2020.FR_.Web_.pdf

73. Ryan, C. L., & Bauman, K. (2016). Educational Attainment in the United States: 2015. Retrieved from http://www.census.gov/content/dam/Census/library/publications/2016/demo/p20-578.pdf

74. Blivin, Jamai, and Ben Wallerstein. "SHIFT HAPPENS - static1.squarespace.com." Shift Happens. Innovate Educate, n.d. Web. 29 Mar. 2017. p 19

75. Ibid

76. https://mscss.us/safety-training/millennials-training/

77. https://www.theatlantic.com/national/archive/2013/05/me-generation-time/315151/

78. http://content.time.com/time/covers/0,16641,19900716,00.html

79. http://web.jobvite.com/Q315_Website_2015RecruiterNation_LP.html

80. http://www.usatoday.com/story/money/markets/2015/08/26/construction-worker-shortage/32430517/

81. http://www.benefitspro.com/2015/07/28/companies-struggle-to-attract-qualified-employees

82. http://offers.indeed.com/rs/699-SXJ-715/images/TalentAttractionStudy.pdf

83. http://cdn.theladders.net/static/images/basicSite/pdfs/TheLadders-EyeTracking-StudyC2.pdf

84. http://www.hronline.com/HRE/view/story.jhtml?id=533345869

85. https://www.recruiter.com/i/5-compelling-statistics-about-recruiting-behavior/

86. http://dhihiringindicators.com/wp-content/uploads/2017/07/2017-06-DHI-Hiring-Indicators-Report-FINAL.pdf

87. http://www.brookings.edu/research/interactives/2014/job-vacancies-and-stem-skills#/M10420

88. http://www.careerbuilder.com/share/aboutus/pressreleases-detail.aspx?sd=12/13/2012&id=pr730&ed=12/31/2012

89. http://hrdailyadvisor.blr.com/2017/03/07/2017-annual-recruiting-survey/

90. http://www.careerxroads.com/aolloquium/files/TheCandidateExperienceMonograph.pdf

91. http://www.glassdoor.com/blog/9-10-job-seekers-search-jobs-mobile-glassdoor-state-mobile-job-search-survey/

92. http://careerbuildercommunications.com/candidatebehavior/

93. http://www.talentmgt.com/articles/build-your-brand-and-candidates-will-follow

94. https://www.appcast.io/mobile_recruiting_guide

95. Ibid.

96. https://www.cornerstoneondemand.com/rework/employee-pursuit-of-purpose

97. Glassdoor U.S. Site Survey, January 2016; *Updated from 94%, Glassdoor survey, October 2014

98. http://pdfserver.amlaw.com/cc/COMMITForumPowerpointdocumentSeptember232013Final.pdf

99. http://www.lehighvalleychamber.org/success-performance-solutions.html

100. https://www.successperformancesolutions.com/recruiting-funnel-works/

101. https://www.appcast.io/mobile_recruiting_guide

102. https://www.cornerstoneondemand.com/re-work/5-tips-managing-unconscious-bias-work

103. http://hrdailyadvisor.blr.com/2015/07/01/the-candi-date-experience-6-facts-every-employer-should-know/

104. https://www.cornerstoneondemand.com/rework/why-ghosting-recruiting-needs-stop

105. http://www.nytimes.com/2015/06/26/fashion/exes-ex-plain-ghosting-the-ultimate-silent-treatment.html

106. http://careerbuildercommunications.com/candidatebehavior/

107. Ibid.

108. http://fortune.com/2015/12/16/job-market-hiring-work-ers/

109. https://www.shrm.org/ResourcesAndTools/hr-topics/tal-ent-acquisition/Pages/Onboarding-Key-Retaining-Engag-ing-Talent.aspx

110. https://insights.moveguides.com/blog/want-the-best-of-the-best-recruit-smarter

111. http://www.leadershipiq.com/blogs/leadership-iq/35354241-why-new-hires-fail-emotional-intelligence-vs-skills

112. http://www.cornerstoneondemand.com/blog/get-board-on-boarding#.ValaMBNViko

113. http://deliberatepractice.com.au/wp-content/up-loads/2013/04/Onboarding-2013.pdf

114. https://www.forbes.com/sites/jjcolao/2013/07/02/who-would-recruit-on-facebook-try-pepsi-gap-aig-and-ora-cle/#57369ee82156

115. https://en.wikipedia.org/wiki/Amazon_Alexa

116. https://hbr.org/2014/09/what-the-companies-that-predict-the-future-do-differently

117. http://www.history.com/this-day-in-history/fords-assembly-line-starts-rolling

118. http://www.history.com/this-day-in-history/ford-motor-company-unveils-the-model-t

119. http://www.history.com/topics/model-t

120. Ibid.

121. https://www.mindtools.com/pages/article/newTMM_Taylor.htm

122. https://www.ibm.com/us-en/marketplace/watson-analytics

123. https://en.wikipedia.org/wiki/watson_(computer)

124. https://www.r-project.org/

125. https://en.wikipedia.org/wiki/Weka_(machine_learning)

126. https://www.thehedgescompany.com/why-job-interviews-are-like-flipping-a-coin/

127. https://www.iperceptions.com/blog/causation-vs-correlation

128. http://joshbersin.com/2016/07/people-analytics-market-growth-ten-things-you-need-to-know/

129. http://www.bersin.com/Lexicon/details.aspx?id=15392

130. https://www.iperceptions.com/blog/causation-vs-correlation

131. https://rework.withgoogle.com/case-studies/Wegmans-conjoint-analysis/

132. https://www.wsj.com/articles/SB124269038041932531

133. http://www.cbsnews.com/news/when-the-robots-take-over-will-there-be-jobs-left-for-us/

134. http://news.harvard.edu/gazette/story/2016/10/the-first-fully-3-d-printed-heart-on-a-chip/

135. https://www.ncbi.nlm.nih.gov/pmc/articles/PMC4437958/

136. http://www.computerworld.com/article/3184834/
healthcare-it/3d-printed-partial-liver-transplants-target-
ed-for-2020.html

137. https://3dprint.com/165822/low-cost-3d-printed-liver-
model/

138. https://www.theverge.com/2016/11/24/13740798/google-
deepmind-ai-lip-reading-tv

139. http://www.zerohedge.com/news/2017-03-04/house-was-
3d-printed-under-24-hours-cost-just-10000

140. https://futurism.com/a-scientist-is-3d-printing-blood-ves-
sels-for-sick-children/

141. http://www.bizjournals.com/sanjose/news/2016/08/30/
how-artificial-intelligence-could-make-you-ceo-of.html

142. https://www.mdtmag.com/news/2017/01/smartphone-sen-
sor-detect-disease-factors-breath

143. https://techcrunch.com/2017/04/07/adidas-latest-3d-
printed-shoe-puts-mass-production-within-sight/

144. http://www.brickmeetsclick.com/alibaba--virtual-reali-
ty--and-online-grocery

145. https://futurism.com/an-ai-completed-360000-hours-of-
finance-work-in-just-seconds/

146. https://www.asianscientist.com/2016/08/topnews/
ibm-watson-rare-leukemia-university-tokyo-artificial-intel-
ligence/

147. https://www.wsj.com/articles/amazon-leans-on-technolo-
gy-to-speed-training-of-holiday-workers-1480329005

148. http://www.repairerdrivennews.com/2016/10/11/trac-
table-ceo-says-ai-will-assess-vehicle-damage-for-mitch-
ell-company-specializes-in-ai-photo-analysis/

149. https://www.technologyreview.com/s/600706/ibms-auto-mated-radiologist-can-read-images-and-medical-records/

150. http://www.npr.org/sections/alltechconsid-ered/2016/08/24/491156218/voice-recognition-software-finally-beats-humans-at-typing-study-finds

151. https://futurism.com/the-relationship-of-the-future-a-man-married-a-robot-he-built-himself/

CPSIA information can be obtained
at www.ICGtesting.com
Printed in the USA
LVOW10s1216291217
561199LV00007B/19/P

9 781628 654646